BOX OF MOONLIGHT & NOTES FROM OVERBOARD

BOX OF MOONLIGHT
&
NOTES FROM OVERBOARD
A Film-Maker's Diary

Tom DiCillo

faber and faber
LONDON · BOSTON

First published in 1997
by Faber and Faber Limited
3 Queen Square London WC1N 3AU

Photoset by Parker Typesetting Service, Leicester
Printed in England by Clays Ltd, St Ives plc

A CIP record for this book
is available from the British Library
ISBN 0-571-19169-X

2 4 6 8 10 9 7 5 3 1

This book is dedicated to Marcus Viscidi, my Producer, Friend and Ally. In the four years it took to make *Box of Moonlight*, he was beside me in the trenches every single day.

A Note About Film Diaries

I doubt anyone will be too distressed to hear but I feel obliged to declare that this is the last film diary I will keep. Furthermore, I caution other film-makers from attempting to write diaries at all.

The experience of making a film is broken into two strictly defined categories: Absolute Elation and Complete Despair. It is impossible to write about the Elation without sounding like a pompous idiot.

'Oh, I did such a great thing on the set today!'

'Oh, the film turned out so great! I am so very, very happy.'

This leaves only the Despair, which for some reason is much easier to write about. Maybe it's because disaster looks better in print.

'Lost all the money today. Filming halted forever.'

'The rejection by Cannes is proving more devastating than I expected. I find I'm shooting heroin of inferior quality more and more frequently.'

In any event, going through the disasters once and then immediately reliving them on paper is starting to smell a bit masochistic to me.

Contents

Notes from Overboard
A Film-Maker's Diary

prologue

During the summer of 1995, I spent three months in Knoxville, Tennessee, directing my third feature, *Box of Moonlight*. It was supposed to have been my second film; the one I'd hoped to make immediately after *Johnny Suede* (1991). The tale of its tortuous journey to celluloid would be of vague interest only to drunken shoe salesmen, stranded in an airport lounge.

In brief, the film was a 'Go Picture' five times. And five times the film fell apart (once two weeks into pre-production). In the months and years between each 'Go Picture' I kept my hopes alive by strenuously imagining myself sitting in some greasy spoon in Knoxville, eating a breakfast of scrambled eggs, grits and a tiny glass of watered-down orange juice. Although I am not fond of these traditional southern breakfasts, I savored this fantasy meal for five years, telling myself, 'Don't give up. One day you will actually be sitting down eating this breakfast and when you are then you will know without a doubt that this film is really getting made.'

However, it wasn't until I had given up making the film completely and made *Living in Oblivion* (about the horrors of making a film) that I finally got the real green light to make *Box of Moonlight*. I arrived in Knoxville in August 1995 to begin pre-production. I chose this small city, nestled in the foothills of the Smoky Mountains, for its tattered, disturbing beauty. Sections of the city seem stopped in time, combining a frontier gothic Americana with a numbing, contemporary blandness, epitomized by endless strips of fast-food suburban wasteland. In contrast, the surrounding countryside is stunningly beautiful: lush rolling hills, spacious forests, meadows, streams and clear blue lakes. I was looking for a landscape that suggested America in a primeval state, before the Europeans arrived. The shoot was exhilarating but brutal – like falling overboard in the Atlantic, in the middle of a hurricane, with fifty-foot waves, 100-mile-an-hour winds and lead shoes. We worked six-day weeks and shot the entire film in thirty-four days. It wasn't until I returned to NY three months later that I realized I never once sat in a greasy spoon and ate a breakfast of scrambled eggs, grits or a tiny glass of watered-down orange juice.

pre-production

Location scouting all day. Found Kid's trailer, an old mobile
home that someone was actually living in up until a year ago. It is
perfectly situated in a clearing, with a grove of trees in the back. It
was bizarre standing in front of it, finally seeing for the first time
what had been real only in my mind, and seemed forever to be an
impossibility.

At 8 p.m., I went to a class C wrestling match at the Knoxville
Coliseum, right across the street from the hotel. I was hoping to
cast some of the wrestlers as Uncle Samson, Saddam Insane and
The InFidel; the three wrestlers Kid watches on his TV. Walked
into an unexpectedly intense dose of contemporary Americana.
Primarily white people, all ages, from the very young to the very
old. Most of the males, boys and men alike, had the same kind of
modern haircut: long on top, shaved to the skull around the sides,
making their heads look like half-peeled potatoes. Made a note to
have Dermot Mulroney's character, Wick, wear a similar haircut.

T-shirt: 'I'm politically incorrect and fuckin' proud of it'.
Another, 'My kid beat up your honor student'. On their way to the
ring the wrestlers walked through a gauntlet created out of
portable metal railings. They were escorted by state troopers in
skin-tight blue uniforms. Teenage girls and small children leaned
over the railings, screaming, taking flash pictures, reaching to
touch the wrestlers as they passed.

Young women in tight tube tops, tiny shorts and pantyhose,
delivered plastic jugs of beer. They were called Hooter Girls
because they all worked at a sportsbar chain called Hooters
featuring waitresses with large breasts. One wrestler got in the ring
and bleated into the microphone, 'Any of you Hooter Girls wants
to go home with a real man tonight just call my name!'

All the teenage girls along the aisle beside me erupted in a
spasm of high-pitched squeals.

One tag-team match was between two beefy, all-American
hunks with long, blond hair, and two scrawny white guys named

PG-13 and NC-17. (These are rating codes for films in the US: Parental Guidance for children under thirteen, and No Children under seventeen.) PG-13 and NC-17 turned the crowd against them by fighting dirty and incensed them further by winning the match. Two fat guys in front of me, dressed completely in biker gear, lurched to their feet and screamed 'No way, man!!' at exactly the same time.

The matches were uniformly dull, however at every pre-choreographed body slam the crowd leapt to its feet with a roar. At one point it seemed to me this utterly fake spectacle of churning emotion and drama was the American working-class equivalent of opera. I found it charming for a few minutes until three guys threatened to punch a woman behind them who'd asked them to sit down.

Outside the arena, sullen, over-weight women sat behind tables selling color photos of the wrestlers in various poses. One photo showed a long-haired wrestler flexing on a small pedestal against a sky-blue background. He was heavily oiled and wore white boots and red satin bikini briefs. Oddly a German shepherd dog was posing on another pedestal beside him. A moment later this wrestler came out in the flesh, wearing the same boots and red briefs, and wrote his name with a black laundry marker on the thin white inner forearms of two teenage girls.

SATURDAY 5 AUGUST   THE DONUT

Driving back from a long day of location scouting with Chip and Nelson, my two location managers. Around 7 p.m. we passed a bright pink strip joint with the word 'Bambi's' painted in six-foot-high black letters on the wall facing the highway. Nelson informed me the place was locally famous for an attraction called the 'Donut Dance'. He did not reveal the details of this dance or how he came to know about it. Thinking it would be a perfect location for the bar where Al and Kid get beaten up, I told Chip to pull over.

Gene, the club's owner, was behind the bar selling Budweiser by the can. He immediately agreed to let us shoot in his parking lot and plunked down three beers, 'on the house'. While he and Chip discussed the details, I took a glance around.

About fifteen men were sitting at tables scattered around a

4

small, elevated runway with a mirrored ball rotating feebly above it. Strangely, the men all looked identical. If most of them weren't sitting alone I would have thought they were members of a family comedy troupe featuring over-weight white guys with long hair, floppy wide-brimmed hats and mirrored sunglasses. They were all staring intently at the limber young blonde who was dancing at the moment, her body moving like a fire hose the firemen have let go of. Off to the side I noticed four or five other dancers, sitting in a quiet cluster, wearing only their bras and G-strings.

As the blonde finished, a hidden male DJ urged the audience into tepid applause by saying, 'OK, that's right, OK, now. Isn't that something? Put your hands together for Tiffany all you gentlemen out there watching these lovely ladies dancing for your pleasure and enjoying pleasing you with their sensuous dancing.'

Tiffany strode up to the bar, refastening her bra behind her as Gene introduced her to us.

'Ain't she sweet? Tiffany just turned twenty-one yesterday. Now she's legal.'

Another blonde in her underwear slid on to the bar stool beside me, introducing herself as Mimi. In contrast to Tiffany, Mimi seemed tired and somewhat nervous. My own uneasiness contributed quite a bit to the dullness of our conversation. I actually heard myself ask her if she had seen any good movies lately. She said she had just taken her two-year-old son to see *Pocahontas* that afternoon.

Just then Tiffany took Nelson's hand and led him to a dark corner of the lounge. They approached a large, white, circular couch with a hole in the center about four feet in diameter. To my amazement, Nelson stepped up on to the seat, put a leg over the back and settled into the hole with only his head protruding.

Then I realized: he was in the Donut. Tiffany removed her bra and commenced what I deduced was the Donut Dance. Essentially this dance consisted of her climbing up on to the circular seatback surrounding the hole, spreading her legs on either side of Nelson's head, and moving her G-stringed pelvis around in front of his face. Nelson appeared quite entranced, though it was somewhat hard to gauge his expression as most of the time his head was completely engulfed by Tiffany's thighs.

At that moment Mimi leaned closer and spoke into my ear. Her breath was warm and scented like baby powder.

'When are you getting in the Donut?' she whispered.

'Oh, not for a while,' I said.

'That's the biggest hole you'll ever be in,' she said.

I turned to her quickly, surprised by her sudden shift to sarcasm. In fact she had been absolutely serious. She wasn't even looking at me. She was staring across the room, watching enviously as Nelson took out his wallet and handed several bills to Tiffany.

As we were driving back to the production office, Nelson quietly asked Chip and I to 'be cool and not go spreading this around'. We assured him that went without saying.

The next morning, as I passed Nelson's office, I saw that someone had already posted a small sign on his door, reading 'Donut Disturb'.

FRIDAY 18 AUGUST

John Turturro and Sam Rockwell arrived this week. Had my first rehearsal with them yesterday, followed by another four-hour session today. Turturro had me immediately on the floor laughing. He jokingly accused me of laughing at my own script; I assured him my laughter was merely my delight at watching him work.

Actually I am delighted my instincts were correct in casting him. I knew I needed an actor of his strength and commitment to pull off some of the more risky moments of humor. In fact, the stronger and more committed he is, the funnier the scene. I told John I wanted him in great shape, suntanned, with impeccable posture. I suggested a combination of a young Burt Lancaster and Ward Cleaver (the father on the fifties TV show *Leave It to Beaver*).

He is gentle and patient with Sam who at the moment is a little nervous. Sam has had the script for so long (four years) that I think he's worked on it too much. He's devised several little actions he plans to do. Some of them are very funny, but some take him out of the scene. I told him if his behavioral ad-libs have nothing to do with intensifying the Kid's interaction with Al, then we're not going to use them.

Sam knocked on my door tonight just as I was getting into bed.

He wanted to show me what he had worked out for the scene after Wick beats him up. He jammed a paper towel into his mouth, explaining that this was to help him suggest 'the whole swollen mouth and broken teeth thing'. Then he did the scene, as if in such agony from the beating he could barely move. The wad of soggy paper towel made his words completely unintelligible.

When he was done I asked him to take the paper towel out of his mouth. I told him it was not a scene about his considerable dexterity in depicting physical pain but about the thrill of revenge.

'Kid is in such an agitated state here that I seriously doubt if he feels any pain at all. Have you ever seen a wild animal with a broken leg? In trying to get away from danger it'll get up and run on it, its fear completely overwhelming its pain. Try it again and this time show me no pain. Just show me how intensely Kid wants to get back at Wick. Show me the thrill he would feel in finally being victorious over him.'

The next time he did it, the speech had a wild, jagged thrust that had me riveted. He left at 1 a.m. We are one week away from shooting.

WEDNESDAY 23 AUGUST

We were scheduled to go up in the helicopter and shoot the Opening aerial shots this week but a low-pressure system settled in, bringing three days of rain. I'd resigned myself to postponing these shots till the end of the shoot when, suddenly today, the weather cleared.

The production team hastily pulled the crew together and about 4.30 p.m. we were in the air. The pilot was Randy Love, a native Tennessean who owned a small sight-seeing business in the foothills of the Smokys. Paul Ryan, our Director of Photography, sat in the front with Randy, operating a nose-mounted camera by remote control. I sat in the back seat with a color video monitor strapped on to my lap.

Randy had a rather perverse sense of humor. While chatting gaily about some friends of his who lived in a school bus below us, he'd turn all the way around in his seat, facing me; seemingly unaware that he was flying straight at the side of a mountain. Just as I was convinced we were all going to die, Randy would laugh and ease the helicopter up a few feet, barely clearing the top of the ridge.

Suddenly he yelled, 'See that house down there?! Watch this; some old guy's gonna come out and wave!'

He banked and dropped the helicopter like a stone, introducing my stomach to the base of my skull. The helicopter skimmed the house so closely one of the struts scraped the stone chimney. Looking over my shoulder as Randy shot straight up in the sky I saw an old man in a sleeveless white T-shirt stagger hurriedly down the cinderblock steps.

'There he is, Tom!' Randy yelled over the roar of the rotor. 'Wave to him!'

I raised my hand in a feeble wave and saw the old man wave frantically back up at us.

The sky had cleared completely. As we headed toward our intended location, the late-afternoon light turned more and more beautiful, bathing the lush green forests and meadows in a rich amber glow. Suddenly I spotted a field of wild soybeans in flower, gleaming bright yellow below us. A small stream meandered through the soybeans, fed by a large blue lake.

I yelled for Randy to turn around, fly low over the lake and skim the field. Paul Ryan began filming as Randy started high over the far end of the lake then dropped lightly to just above the surface and sped toward land. In the distance I saw a group of trees with an opening in the middle, almost like a gateway to another world.

'Go through the trees!' I yelled. I watched transfixed through the monitor as the sparkling water rushed past beneath us. Randy guided the helicopter effortlessly through the opening in the trees then immediately began following the stream that flowed through the yellow soybeans. A lone bird broke into flight ahead of us, leaving staggered ripples in the turquoise water. As we kept flying, sustaining the shot for over two minutes, a euphoria came over me that was so exhilarating it made me laugh out loud. By complete accident we had stumbled upon the perfect place, on the perfect day, at the perfect time. I couldn't believe we were actually getting this on film.

I have the opening of the film. With the right music, these images will immediately pull the audience into the beautiful, mysterious world I hope to create.

shooting

First day of shooting. Last night I had two calls from executive
producers 'just calling to wish me good luck' at 12.30 a.m. It was a
little difficult to fully appreciate their graciousness, especially since
I'd gone to bed at 10 p.m. in preparation for my 5 a.m. call time.

On set, I was so groggy I barely knew what I was saying. But the
shooting went well; we finished all of the bus shots, interior and
exterior. Had an unexpected argument with Turturro after our last
shot. I listened carefully to his complaint, judged it to be
unfounded, and called it a 'wrap'. He walked away, still angry.
An hour later I met him coming into the hotel and we worked it
out.

He is a tough one to read. At times he is amazingly warm,
supportive and giving. During his swimming lesson yesterday, he
took off his ring and set it by the edge of the pool. It was slightly
larger than his finger and he was afraid it might come off in the
water. His father had given it to him shortly before he died and he
valued it greatly. While he was swimming someone stole the ring.
As distraught as he was, he continued the lesson.

The film calls for him to jump into a pool of water and swim
leisurely, speaking several lines of dialogue. John never learned to
swim and is a little uneasy being in water over his head. The
swimming instructor spent most of the lesson yesterday showing
him how to hold his breath. Physically he looks great; slim,
tanned, muscular; amazingly similar to photos of my father as a
young man.

Originally, the location for the swimming hole was to be a small
mountain stream. But I had problems finding one deep enough
and ultimately scrapped the whole idea because in every one of the
streams the rushing water was freezing and very loud. Last week
we decided on an abandoned rock quarry. This solves a lot of
problems. It's quiet. The water is warm and we can shoot on our
own time, unimpeded by the public.

On the down side, the water is 350 feet deep. I'd originally told

Turturro, on the basis of the mountain stream concept, that the maximum depth would never exceed six feet. He asked me today how deep the quarry was and I said, 'Twenty-five feet, in some places.' Which is not strictly a lie. I've instructed everyone on the film to repeat exactly the same thing if asked.

Matters were not helped by a headline yesterday in the local newspaper: EXPERT SWIMMER DROWNS IN QUARRY. The details were pretty gruesome. The rescue diver who brought him up from the bottom of the quarry discovered the victim had first been bitten by a poisonous snake.

SUNDAY 10 SEPTEMBER
Just finished second week of shooting. The intensity of the work is unending. Every day accelerates into a wild, chaotic scramble as we try to get the shots before the light goes. Turturro is having more and more consistent moments of brilliance. His concentration is staggering. He agreed with a note I gave him that the vocal inflection he was using tended to deflate Al's energy and make him too tortured. It's a hard, thin line for us both to walk. While I never want Al's turmoil to be depressing to the audience, it still has to be real for John.

In the film, Al returns to Splatchee Lake, a water park he had visited as a child. He discovers it is now in ruins and shares his memories with Luvven and Wynelle Coddle, two elderly strangers strolling along the polluted shoreline. We shot all the Coddles' coverage first then turned around for John's coverage in the afternoon. I only told him one thing: 'Convince these two that nothing is bothering you.'

It is immediately apparent when one of my suggestions stimulates John. He jumped up and said, 'OK, OK, let's go!' From the opening moment of the shot Turturro was like a living man right in front of us. The pretext of small-talk suggested in my note actually prompted him to dig deeper into the emotion of the scene. The story he was telling became so convincing that Luvven and Wynelle, though off-camera, were laughing and reacting like no one was at the lake but the three of them.

As he neared the end of the scene John trembled and his eyes filled with tears. I was staring, transfixed. Out of the corner of my eye I suddenly saw the Assistant Cameraman look at the footage

11

counter and shake his head. John was about to finish the last few lines of the scene when I heard the camera quietly run out of film. The AC glanced at me in question. I shook my head and continued, as if we were still filming. When John finished the scene I yelled, 'Cut!' We did several more takes. Fortunately John filled the last moments of the scene again in these later takes. I did not tell him about the camera running out of film until the end of the day.

SUNDAY 17 SEPTEMBER
The pace is taking its toll. Turturro is yelling at people. I am yelling at people. Yesterday Turturro yelled at me. During the swimming hole scene where Al and Kid meet Floatie and Purlene (played by Catherine Keener and Lisa Blount), I asked Turturro to quicken the pace by walking over some rocks. He stumbled during the shot then went on to finish the scene. As soon as I yelled 'cut' he exploded. He'd broken two toes. My sole directorial accomplishment for the rest of the day was to keep him from flying back to New York. When we resumed shooting the next morning, his toes were the size and color of two small eggplants. Nonetheless, he did all of his swimming scenes with no outward signs of nervousness. He never asked me how deep the quarry was.

Walkie-talkies keep going off right in the middle of the most delicate dialogue scenes. I told the AD I was very upset about this and nearly went insane when I heard him reply, 'Well now, you know, Tom, these things are inevitable.'

My response, indicating precisely where on his anatomy the next walkie-talkie would end up, appeared to have some effect. There were no walkie squawks during shooting for the next six days.

For four years the opening line of the script has read, 'Camera emerges from foliage into a clearing to reveal a wide-eyed, ceramic Bambi.' All during pre-production I stressed to the Art Department that I wanted 'a ceramic Bambi, a fawn right out of a Walt Disney cartoon'.

Yesterday we set up for the two shots involving this ceramic Bambi. Just before we were to shoot I walked past the Art Department van and jumped suddenly, seeing a real deer, an adult

12

doe, nosing in the grass behind the van. It took several moments for me to realize it was fake and several more to realize this was the 'ceramic Bambi' the Art Department had produced. There was nothing cartoonish about it at all. It was not Bambi, it was a real deer, a plastic hunter's decoy.

My infuriated confusion was met by profuse apologies from the Art Department. After weeks of searching, this deer was the closest they could come to 'a wide-eyed ceramic Bambi'. As we had one hour of daylight left to shoot two lengthy scenes I made the decision to shoot with the new deer.

Halfway through filming the scene where Al walks up to the deer and thumps it in surprise, saying, 'It's a fake! It's a statue!' I suddenly realized that this realistic-looking deer was actually perfect for the scene. If it had been a cartoon Bambi, Al would never have thought it was real, even from afar. Which placed me in a particularly paralysing dilemma. Part of me wanted to rage at the Art Department for not getting me the ceramic Bambi specified in the script. The other part of me wanted to hug them all in desperate gratitude for saving the scene.

TUESDAY 19 SEPTEMBER

In the script, I'd indicated that one of Kid's hubcaps falls off and rolls down the street as he and Al pull into the rental car parking lot. Although a small detail, I'd attached a lot of importance to it, both as a symbol of Kid's character and as a premonition of something he says later in the film.

A week into pre-production I had a meeting with Orvis, the prop man, about how to do this. I told him how important it was to me and he assured me that although getting the hubcap to fly off a spinning wheel on cue might be complicated, it could be done. A week before shooting he informed me he was still working on it. Today, as we were setting up the shot, Orvis informed me with grave sincerity that the effect was impossible. After listening to his detailed explanations as to why every one of his ideas had proved unsuccessful, I told the camera grips to strap me on to the back of the car and I would throw the hubcap off myself.

Eventually dissuaded from doing this, I started filming, resigned to the fact that I was not going to get my hubcap flying off. We started the shot. The convertible emerged from a side road and began crossing the highway. Sam was a little nervous driving and made the turn too fast. The car hit a small bump and to my astonished delight, the lone hubcap facing the camera flew off. I gaped like a happy idiot as it rolled along with the car for a few feet then fell on its side with a clatter. Every other disappointment on the film instantly disappeared in the face of this miracle.

Just as I was about to scream in joyful delirium the AC yelled, 'Camera jam! Got to cut!'

As I watched in shock, he snapped open the camera door and a long accordion of bent, twisted film sprang out. The camera had stopped just after the hubcap fell off, rendering the shot unusable. After a month of shooting, after running over 80,000 feet of film without a single snag, the camera jammed right at this particular moment. It was a karmic joke of such enormous skill I was crushed into speechless awe and humility. I tried to laugh. I give myself credit for that.

THURSDAY 21 SEPTEMBER

My wife, Jane, flew down for the weekend. I feel like it's been twenty years since I last saw her. Her visit was very sweet, though we spent most of the few hours we were together discussing my frustration. As usual, her advice and encouragement were astute. 'You are the captain of the ship,' she said. 'Whether you like it or not, you are responsible for everything.'

'Broken toes? Hubcaps?' I asked.

'Everything. The sooner you accept this, the better off you'll be.'

She flew back to NY this morning. When I got back from dailies tonight at twelve, I found a note she left me. Inside was a drawing of me on a boat in the middle of the ocean. The word 'action' was coming out of my mouth. Although the drawing was meant to be constructive, portraying me as 'captain of the ship', I couldn't help noticing that I was alone on the boat, which looked alarmingly like a rudderless toy and none too seaworthy. I also noticed the waves were approaching tsunami height and seemed about to crush the boat and wash me overboard.

MONDAY 25 SEPTEMBER

Just finished a week of night shooting at Kid's trailer. The location was in lush farmland with only a few widely interspersed houses.

15

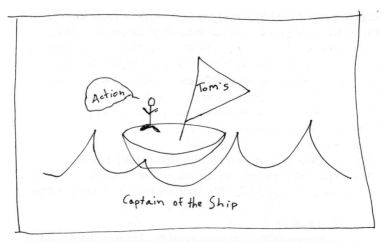

Captain of the Ship

Our base camp was on the front lawn of one of these houses, about half a mile from the set. On our first night, just after the sun went down, I went into Turturro's trailer for a little pep talk. I apologized for the irritating delays that were occurring on the set. Just the day before he'd blown up at the lighting crew when we stopped for half an hour to relight after doing one take. 'You guys have three hours to light this shot. I'd like to do two takes in row without having to stop!'

He's right. There is a disturbing lack of focus on the set, particularly from the Camera and Lighting Departments. Last week we had to redo three shots because someone had forgotten to turn the key light back on after taking a light reading.

I assured Turturro that I had spoken to the department heads and there would be no delays tonight. We had eight pages of dialogue to shoot. I told him we had fresh 1000-foot magazines and therefore wouldn't have to stop to reload after every take. He was in good spirits; we joked a little and before I left he thanked me for my concern.

I opted to walk to the set instead of being driven. It was a beautiful clear evening, cool, with stars beginning to glint in the darkening blue sky. I used the walk as an attempt to rekindle my own sputtering enthusiasm for the film.

I was the captain of the ship. If my mood was dark, sullen and tinged with futility, this would affect the entire film. At a bend in

16

the road I saw the multi-colored strings of lights from Kid's trailer glowing like jewels in the darkness. I made a vow to myself right then, that no matter what happened I would be positive; I would be . . . well, positive was all I could think of. I mentally placed myself in a 'tense moment' and imagined myself laughing in the face of adversity.

I walked on to the set, lined up the first shot with Paul Ryan, the DP, then stood shooting the bull with Tip and Raynor, the first and second ACs.

'So, we've got enough film for tonight?' I asked jokingly.

The sudden ripple of alarm that passed over Raynor's face stilled my jovial mood immediately. Raynor spoke quietly to Tip for a moment.

'What's going on?' I asked.

Tip turned to me. 'I don't know how this happened,' he said, 'but we've only got short-ends' (left-over film from longer rolls).

It wasn't really adversity yet but I laughed anyway. 'That's funny,' I said, realizing he was pulling my leg. 'You had me for a moment.'

'No, it's true,' Raynor whispered with a panic that was unmistakable. 'Someone forgot to order the 1000-foot loads. We've only got a few short-ends left. I'm not even sure it's enough to get through the night.'

A moment later I was 500 yards into the woods staring in stunned agony at the tree that had almost broken my foot just because I'd kicked it with all my might. When I returned, Marcus Viscidi, my Producer, friend and ally, was in the middle of a terse meeting with all the members of the Camera Department. It was true; at 7.30 p.m., on the first night of a week of night shooting, it was discovered that someone (no one knew precisely who) had forgotten to order the film. Marcus sent a PA immediately on a three-hour trip to Nashville to pick up a supply of film. In the meantime we'd have to shoot with the short-ends; which meant stopping to reload after every take.

I walked back up the road to Turturro's trailer, dragging my rekindled enthusiasm behind me like a dead rat on a string. I told Turturro what had happened. To my astonishment, he took the news calmly and seemed more concerned about my own state of mind which was hovering between mass-murder and suicide.

17

We went back down to the set and started shooting, stopping after each two-minute take to reload. The fresh 1000-foot loads arrived sometime after 2 a.m., with the last short-end in the camera. We shot till dawn. When a 'wrap' was called I was surprised to hear the crew break into applause. We'd shot all of the eight pages.

The following night we shot the scene where Al and Kid return to the trailer after being beaten up by Wick. This was the scene Sam had brought to my hotel room over a month ago; we hadn't worked on or spoken about it since. Sam was extremely agitated, knowing this was a critical scene. If he did not peel himself raw, it would not work. If he played the end of the scene (collapsing in Turturro's arms), the scene would have nowhere to go. I also knew if we didn't get it on the first take, we'd probably never get it. I said nothing to Sam while Make-up applied the gashes and fake blood to him and Turturro.

I told the Camera and Sound Departments to be absolutely sure they were ready. As soon as the make-up was on we were going for a take and I wanted nothing to interrupt it. When the last smear of blood was on Sam's face I pulled him aside quickly and said, 'Here's all I want you to do. Take every ounce of frustration, anger, fury that's built up in you over this entire film and put it

into this moment. Fury at me, fury at John; I know it's there. Do not go into his arms until he makes you.'

Before he could answer, I ran back to the camera and called 'action'.

The scene was remarkable. Sam's speech about getting revenge on Wick was focused and precise, with none of the distracting physical mannerisms he'd brought into my hotel room. When he realized Al wasn't going to help him, Sam suddenly erupted and began flailing wildly at Turturro, who stayed with him, stayed in the scene and slowly, steadfastly, calmed him down. Finally, Sam broke into tears and collapsed into Turturro's arms.

The AD was horrified we weren't going to do it again, seemingly unaware this was the first time he'd encouraged me to do another take during the entire film. I said no, and we moved on to coverage of the scene. I must admit it's a little frightening knowing this exquisite moment only exists on a single piece of film. A scratch on the negative, a screw-up in the lab and it's disaster.

The next three nights were spent shooting the Fireworks Sequence and the Dancing Scene. I wanted the Fireworks Scene to feel home-made, slightly cheap but very personal; very American. To that end, I made sure the fireworks we used were not overly spectacular and I had Sam shoot them off in unconventional ways: bouncing them off trees, shooting them into the open door of an abandoned kitchen stove. Deglamorizing them made it seem more like the event that millions of people have experienced year after year, in their own backyards.

Originally, the script had indicated that Al, Kid, Floatie and Purlene strip down to their underwear and dance around the fire. At the last minute I changed the dancing to jumping, thinking the images of near-naked bodies passing through flames would be more poetic.

Then, two days ago, Turturro was goofing around between takes and he started dancing the way he imagined Al would dance; a tight, spastic twitch that was hilarious. I immediately decided to go back to the dancing idea.

Nonetheless, I was still nervous about the scene. If the actors held back, if they didn't commit to it entirely, it would fall flat and would end up looking more than a little stupid. I chose 'Carioca' an instrumental by The Fireballs, a pre-surf band I'd discovered researching music for *Johnny Suede*. I was so convinced this tune was going in the final film I had Marcus get the rights to it before we started filming. Usually these scenes are filmed silent, the actors faking like they're dancing so their dialogue and actions can be recorded cleanly by the Sound Man. The actual music is only laid in at the final mix.

This dancing to nothing can be very awkward and embarrassing for the actors. To the Sound Man's horror, I plugged in a big boom box and told the actors we were going for it live. I cranked the music up as loud as it would go and we started filming.

Turturro leapt at this chance for pure physical activity. His wild enthusiasm spurred Catherine, Sam and Lisa to go wild on their own. When the song ended the crew applauded. Then we shot it five more times, and each time all four actors gave it everything.

Got back to the hotel just as the sun was coming up. I stood at my window in blissful exhaustion watching it, crimson and as bright as Day-Glo paint, rise slowly through the thick, white fog covering the Tennessee River below me.

WEDNESDAY 27 SEPTEMBER
Catherine Keener appeared and disappeared like a brief flash of sun on a dreary day. Her performance as Floatie was as magical and effervescent as anything she's ever done. Everyone misses her.

Had an odd experience filming her phone-sex scene. We constructed a tiny set for her 'office' and spent a rare day shooting indoors. At one point I looked up and saw her sitting there on that tiny, fake set, surrounded by lights, the camera and the boom operator hovering with the mike just out of frame. Just then Catherine glanced up and smiled at me. In that instant I had a sudden rush of memory of filming *Living in Oblivion*: the joyful carelessness, the intimacy, the comforting, insular world created by that clan of crazy, trusting friends. I valued it then. I treasure it now.

Dermot will stay another two weeks to finish his last two scenes. His prosthetic burn looks startlingly realistic. He liked my idea of the haircut shaved to the scalp around the sides. He's come up with some physical actions that work well for Wick; an odd, bow-legged strut and a compulsion to always be eating ice of some kind.

The last night Catherine was here, she, Dermot and I went out to dinner. The young waitress recognized Dermot and asked for his autograph. 'You were like, good friends with River Phoenix, weren't you?'

'Yes, I was,' Dermot replied. He and River had grown extremely close following the film they did together, *A Thing Called Love.*

'Oh, that's like excellent.' A tight, nervous giggle. 'Were you, like, really bummed when he died?'

'I was pretty upset,' Dermot answered quietly, with a restraint that astonished me and sky-rocketed my respect for him. My impulse would have been to take my butter knife and tattoo the word 'bummed' across her forehead.

SUNDAY I OCTOBER

Filmed the Tomato Field sequence yesterday. This included the Tomato Fight between Al and Kid, and the scene where Kid pushes the police car down a hill. Started shooting at first light and ended in a frantic rush to get the last shot as the sun went down. Should have had at least two days to film this sequence. The Tomato Fight itself took over two hours to choreograph. We shot the whole thing with a Steadicam in a series of long, uninterrupted takes. The heat was intense. Sam was exhausted after the first take, running full tilt in his heavy buckskin costume. Again, Turturro plunged into this physical activity and he just kept going. He had a wickedly accurate aim, nailing Sam repeatedly with hard, straight shots from all the way across the field.

In a medium shot of Turturro, we needed to have a big tomato hit him right in the chest, as if Kid had thrown it from off-camera. A prop girl stood a few feet away and hurled several wet, mushy tomatoes at John, missing each time. John had requested she do it, 'because it will be more humiliating to have a woman hit me'. After the fourth miss I grabbed two tomatoes and said, 'Alright, I'm doing this.'

As I aimed at John standing three feet away, I heard someone mutter, 'A pretty accurate representation of the relationship between Director and Actor.'

My first shot missed John completely. My second hit him hard in the shoulder, raising a welt the size of a pancake.

The runaway police car was a complicated set-up involving a stunt driver steering the car straight at the backs of the Sheriff and Patrolman, who were actors and had to jump out of the way at the right time. My excitement at shooting my first real movie stunt was obliterated by my conviction that someone would die because we were all running around like frenzied lunatics on speed.

We used three cameras (the third operated by one of the truck drivers), which only complicated matters and created three times as much yelling because each camera seemed unable to set up a shot without both the other cameras in frame.

The tomato field belonged to Wagner Forelock, a gracious and dignified older man with wavy white hair and a small white mustache. I'd invited him to watch us filming. He stayed out there all day, along with his wife and son.

At the end of the day I dragged myself into the front seat of the crew van, about to depart, and was almost asleep when I saw Wagner Forelock standing in front of his house with his wife, son and some neighbors. I got out and thanked Wagner for his hospitality. Oddly he barely shook my hand and did not look me in the eye. Alarmed, I asked him what the matter was. After a heavy sigh he turned to me and said, 'I like you, Tom, but I have to tell you I won't be able to recommend this movie to my friends.'

'Why not?' I asked.

'The language.'

I racked my brain trying to recall some vulgarity Sam or John may have screamed during the tomato fight.

'What language?' I asked finally. 'Did someone on the crew say something?'

Wagner sighed again. 'No, Tom, it was the Sheriff. He used the Lord's name in vain. He said, "Jesus, we killed 'em." Do you remember?'

I nodded in astonishment as he went on.

'You see, Tom, Jesus is my dearest, closest friend. Jesus is my light and my life. And you used his name in a bad way. And now I won't be able to tell my friends to see this movie or go see it myself. I like you and I don't hold it against you, but these are my beliefs and I take them very seriously.'

It really bothered me that I had caused him such distress. I told him I respected his beliefs and I would never in any way want to insult him or cast aspersions on his spiritual convictions. In conclusion I told him how sorry I was that we had to end our brief relationship on a note of disappointment.

'It's OK, Tom,' he said, putting his arm around me. 'I'll tell you what; to prove there's no hard feelings, let me show you something inside.'

As he led me into the house, I glanced back at the waiting crew van. Everyone inside was glaring at me in vexed exhaustion, wanting to get the hell out of there. At that moment there was nothing I wanted more than to be inside that van.

Inside the small house, Wagner opened a door and ushered me into a dark room, whispering confidentially, 'This is where we make our own Smoky Mountain BBQ sauce.'

A huge stainless-steel vat stood gleaming in the center of the room. Wagner pointed to it proudly and said, 'That's where it happens, right there, in my brand-new vat. It holds eighty-five gallons.'

'*Jesus!* You're kidding me!' I blurted in amazement. The silence that filled the tiny room was endless and excruciating. Finally Wagner turned away and led me back outside. I crawled into the van and waved goodbye to him as we pulled out. In the side-view mirror I saw Wagner say something to his wife with a slow, sad shake of his head.

SUNDAY EVENING. 8 OCTOBER

Finished the week in a supermarket parking lot shooting the scene where Jesus appears on a hamburger billboard. We had about 200 extras, cop cars, news vans, TV crews. My anxiety about dealing with all these elements was further complicated by the presence of my parents. They'd made the two-hour drive from their home in North Carolina to spend the day with me and witness a film being shot.

I'd never had my parents on set before and for the first hour even the simplest decisions became quagmires of impossibility. I kept expecting to hear my father yell at me, 'Hey! What are you doing here?! You should be home, mowing the lawn!'

Eventually I calmed down and even put them in the foreground of a wide shot of the crowd gazing up at the billboard hamburger.

I was very impressed when my father (an avowed agnostic and ex-catholic) started genuflecting somberly while my mother began taking pictures of the sign with the camera she'd brought.

While I was setting up for another shot, I saw Turturro walk over and stand chatting with my parents for some time. They'd met once before in NYC at the *Living in Oblivion* première. Unknown to my father, John and I had based some of Al's character on him; in particular his posture and semi-military bearing. As they stood next to each other, I was startled to see how similar they looked, almost like the same man, only one was forty years older.

Went to a local supermarket this evening at 8.30. On the way out I was met by a homely, obese white woman in her thirties, dressed in a knitted sweatsuit gray with age and grime. She shook a can at me that contained several coins and said, 'Can you help my daughter win the Homecoming Princess?'

Glancing behind her, I saw a little girl, about nine, short, fat and despite her delighted grin, painfully unattractive. She held a ragged black and white pompom in her hand and as her mother said 'Homecoming Princess' she raised the pompom and shook it once.

I realized suddenly the help her mother wanted from me was not advice about posture or grooming but money. After dropping some coins in her can, I moved away but turned back to look, still somewhat amazed. Just then an old man came out of the store. The mother shook her can, the little fat girl shook the pompom and the old man dropped a coin in the can with a clink. As he walked off he exclaimed loudly, 'Good luck, and I hope she wins!'

'Oh she will,' the mother called back. 'She's talented. It's only money is all she needs.'

THURSDAY 12 OCTOBER

Finished shooting the film at 9 a.m., about two hours ago. What day is it? When did this day begin? Hard to recall. I've been up for twenty-eight hours. Started yesterday with pick-up shots for some daytime exteriors, then the whole company moved to the parking lot at Bambi's Bar to shoot the fight scene. We started as soon as it was dark and worked steadily through the night.

The scene was short but complicated. Wick and his partner

Doob, get out of their truck and move to enter the bar. Passing Al and Kid, someone throws a match at Wick who immediately assumes it was Kid and punches him hard in the face. As Al moves to help Kid, Doob punches him in the stomach then smashes his head against a car headlight. While Al is stretched out on the pavement Wick props up the nearly unconscious Kid and knees him hard in the face. The fake blood was so realistic that at one point I glanced at Sam sprawled on his back with his eyes closed and jumped because he looked like he was dead.

Around 4 a.m. the AD whispered in my ear that we'd just shot Turturro's last shot. I told him to make the announcement to the company and waited for the applause to end with a rising apprehension. The last few days have been tense for both of us. Suddenly, however, as Turturro walked toward me I was startled by an intense rush of emotion. He had given the role everything, there was no question of that. And there was also no question he would be brilliant in the film. But the toll was enormous. As he got closer I suddenly recalled my first letter to him, two years ago, in which I'd urged him, in naked desperation, to read my script.

Then we embraced and he was gone. It struck me again, the only constant in this business is the continuous cycle of drawing together and breaking apart.

A half-hour later Dermot was gone. Then Sam. I got fake blood all over me as we said goodbye. It was still pitch black outside when we moved inside Bambi's to do the last shot of the film; a slow-motion shot of a gray hair falling to the floor. Although it was only a brief, locked off camera shot, it was still quite complicated and tedious. I had several sizes and shapes of hair to decide upon, in addition to getting the hair to fall at the right speed and land at the right spot.

As Orvis, the prop man, stood dropping single gray hairs in the dead silence of the closed bar, I looked up and saw that Orvis, the DP and myself were the only ones awake. All around us in the darkness, on the floor, on tables, on the white circular donut couch, the entire crew was asleep. At that instant my own exhaustion washed over me like a gigantic wave and almost pounded me to sleep on my feet.

Sometime later, we finished the shot and the film was over. I walked around like a zombie shaking people's hands and thanking

them. Someone handed me a plastic cup of champagne and after two sips I was completely wasted. I staggered out of the bar and was dumbfounded to see the sun was already over the trees at the far end of the parking lot, shining pale and diffused through the thin mist that was hanging in the air. I sat down on a camera case lying on the cracked sidewalk in front of the bar. The film was over.

Out in the parking lot the equipment trucks were being loaded. Two grimy electricians paused after coiling a mound of cable to exchange phone numbers. A wardrobe assistant walked by carrying Kid's blood-stained buckskin costume in one hand and a cup of champagne in the other. Someone in the camera truck turned on a radio, low, and the faint music seemed to rise and mingle with the pale yellow mist. The film was over.

post-production

Sitting on the plane at London Heathrow, waiting for take-off on
the flight back to NYC. Arrived in London the morning of the
fifth, presented *Living in Oblivion* at the London Film Festival in
the afternoon. Started interviews for the British release the next
morning at 10 a.m. Flew to Dublin at 5 p.m. Started Irish press
today at 10 a.m., flew back to Heathrow at 6 p.m. and here I am.

Rabin was assassinated the morning I arrived. None of the
journalists who interviewed me mentioned this. I didn't mention it
either. Apparently reality has no place in the world of
entertainment.

Box of Moonlight is inching into life on the editing table. I'm
meeting Camilla Toniolo in the editing room tomorrow at 1 p.m.
She's been cutting since we started shooting and is close to having
a rough cut ready. The three months of shooting *Box of Moonlight*
in Knoxville have already slipped into a vague blend of dream and
memory.

Crossing the ego minefields was more exhausting than the
physical demands of shooting. The levels of diplomacy I had to
engage in have made me unable to discern the difference between
being flexible, being rigid and being shat upon. Several people
have tried to steer me toward a more optimistic view lately. They
say, 'In the end, Tom, *YOU* won. You got the movie, you got the
scenes, the acting, the shots, you got everything the way you
wanted. No matter what you went through, in the end you won.'

Marcus told me last week he loves the result of our hard work
but expressed a disillusionment similar to mine. Faced now with
another round of Pin the Tail on the Donkey with critics and
distributors, our accomplishment seems inconsequential. I did say
to Marcus that at least we are proud of the film we just made.
Imagine going through this hell for something you felt was a piece
o'shit.

I brought *The Philosophy of Andy Warhol* for airplane reading.
Warhol writes that he's an Artist Businessman and proud of it.

Interestingly, every distributor I've met has gone out of their way to stress that they are not just Businessmen, but Lovers of Film. In fact, they almost seem ashamed of their business skills. They claim that whatever business skills they have are only used Artistically; to nurture, protect and prolong the release of Your Film. But, ultimately they are Businessmen and everyone would be better off if they just admitted it. They toss Your Film into the sales bin and wait to see if anybody notices it. If no one does, they wait a little while and very courteously throw another film in on top of it, diverting their Artistic Acumen to their Next Acquisition.

FRIDAY 17 NOVEMBER

Back in NYC. Had a lunch meeting with Bart Walker, an agent at ICM. He wanted to talk to me about leaving William Morris. Not the best kind of discussion to have with a hangover.

Bart was serious about wanting to represent me. He has an impressive client list that includes several independent film-makers. His aim is to help his clients retain as much artistic control as possible, and he did this by creating different financing strategies for them. I told him from my experience financing independent films is a very competitive endeavor. The money sources are few and limited. I asked him what he would do if all of his clients had projects they were trying to finance at the same time. If I signed with him, would I have to worry about which of his independent directors would get priority? Which script would he pitch first, which one would he pitch hardest? Walker said that wasn't the way he worked and he assured me that every director and every script is handled with special care. Anyway, I think that's what he said; the hangover found its second wind right then.

Left the meeting resolved to stay with William Morris for the time being.

Went down to Tribeca to see a new play Jim Farmer had written and directed. Jim composed the score for both *Johnny Suede* and *Living in Oblivion*. We've talked about him scoring *Box of Moonlight*. While waiting for the play to begin I overheard two women behind me reading through the playbill.

'Oh, he did the music for *Johnny Suede*.'

'I didn't see it.'

29

'Not bad. And look here, he did the music for *Living in Oblivion* too.'

'I think I saw that.'

'Not bad either.'

It was a little unnerving hearing six years of my life discussed so perfunctorily.

The play was hilarious; a cross between the Marx Brothers, Kafka and *Leave It to Beaver*. Congratulated Jim afterwards but left on an awkward note. Lakeshore Entertainment, the executive producers of *Box of Moonlight*, has been pressuring me to hire a composer with more recognizable credits than Jim's. It was very hard to tell him that there was some question whether he would be doing the music for *Box of Moonlight*.

TUESDAY 21 NOVEMBER
Screened the rough cut on the Steenbeck this morning at 9.30. We watched it non-stop. As soon as reel one was over, Keiko and Sandra, Camilla's two assistants, jumped up and changed reels like a pit crew in an auto race. The four of us were the only ones in the room. It took almost three hours.

The movie unfolds like a strange Chinese box. It has moments of beauty, humor and surprisingly affecting emotion. It has a somewhat magical quality, like a contemporary *Wizard of Oz*, only more frayed around the edges. Sam Rockwell comes off very well. He more than holds his own against Turturro, who is magnificent.

The material, however, is very dense. It will take excruciating care to extract the film. Music is crucial. Some scenes cannot be cut until the music is chosen or composed.

Afterwards, I took Camilla and her staff out for lunch. In the bathroom I caught a glimpse of my face in the mirror. I looked exhausted, dark circles under my eyes, my face lined. I've aged five years in the last three months.

THANKSGIVING DAY
Egon Friske's name has come up as a composer that would satisfy both Lakeshore and me. I've known him for over ten years, but have never worked with him as a composer. He's got several large films to his credit and I think his sensibility might be right for *Box of Moonlight*. I called him and asked if he was even interested. He hinted that he might be but wondered if we would 'bump heads'.

I said, 'I'd be hiring you because of your talent. Once we agree on what the film is about, I'm going to leave you alone.'

Egon hemmed and hawed about the money but said he'd think about it. I've decided I won't hire him unless he really wants to do it. If he's not completely committed, I'll give it to Jim Farmer.

SATURDAY 25 NOVEMBER

Had some fun today, cutting the first Driving Montage using 'Wayward Nile', an instrumental by the Chantays. The piece may not be new, but the reverb and the Middle Eastern lilt in the melody give it a mysterious beauty that feels perfect for the film. It's extremely emotional and evokes the uneasy lure of the open road.

After work, Jane and I went to see *Leaving Las Vegas*. I must admit, I found it somewhat confusing and kept whispering to Jane, 'What's going on?' A guy meets a beautiful prostitute who loves him unconditionally, gives a great blowjob, can cook brown rice and he still can't lighten up. I guess the film was saying he's better off dead.

MONDAY 27 NOVEMBER

Just called Jim Farmer and told him I was hiring Egon Friske to do the music. It was a very tough call. In addition to being a good friend, Jim has created two beautiful scores for me, for practically nothing. I explained that due to the larger scope of *Box of Moonlight*, Lakeshore was urging me to try a composer with a little more experience. He was extremely gracious and assured me that although he was disappointed he understood my need to work with other people.

I think my decision is correct. But despite Jim's gallantry I know it hurt him and I hung up feeling considerably less than gleeful. I hate the silent brutality that permeates this business.

MONDAY 4 DECEMBER

Went into the editing room early this morning and worked more on the towing sequence where Kid tows Al's car back to his trailer. Feeling the time crunch. Supposedly we are on a schedule of two reels a day. Now that we've spent a day and a half on a two-minute sequence we have to race to catch up. Unfortunately, the difference that perfecting one cut makes is astounding, which makes it hard to move on until every cut is right. I want the film to be in the best possible shape for the Cannes selection committee in April.

Broke away at one for lunch with Carl and Craig, two William Morris agents assigned to work with me here in NY. Although both were pleasant enough there were several weighty lags in the conversation. After one particularly lengthy one, Carl coughed lightly and asked, 'So, are you going away for Christmas?' Another lull ensued a few moments later, after which Carl swallowed and asked, 'So, do you live in the Village?'

Went back to editing room and worked until six on the rest of reel four. Nearly fell asleep on the train coming home. Walked in, said 'hi' to Jane, then collapsed on the bed and slept for twenty minutes. A dog lunging at me woke me from a dream.

TUESDAY 5 DECEMBER
Into the editing room at one. Worked extensively on the arrival at Kid's, particularly the revealing of the open back side of his trailer. Then spent the rest of the day on the scene in Lyle's garage, where Al witnesses Kid's first encounter with Wick. During a break in the cutting, I went up to the Effects Room with Keiko, Camilla's assistant. We needed several crucial sounds to help pace some of the scenes: gunshots, tire squeals, phone rings and birds flying.

After we had finished transferring most of the effects, Keiko reviewed her list and said with quiet efficiency, 'Oh, yes. And we need one fart.' Frank, the engineer performing the transfers, solemnly punched up 'fart' on the computer and a moment later a list of fart sound effects appeared on the screen. 'Wet slapper. Loud dry fart. Short dribbler. High-pitched fart. Low, wet corker.' After listening carefully to them all, I chose the 'Low, wet corker'.

We took the tape back down to the editing room and gave it to Camilla to cut into the sound track. At one point she held up the piece of 35mm film strip and, waving it around, asked, 'Is this it? Are these nine frames the fart?' By this time Keiko was laughing so hard she had tears in her eyes. I was on my hands and knees.

WEDNESDAY 6 DECEMBER
Slept badly. I guess I was anxious about meeting Charlie Flax today, a famous actor who had seen *Living in Oblivion* and told my agents he'd like to meet me. I've only seen one of his movies,

about six years ago. I kept waking up all night wondering what I was going to say to him about all the films he's been in since that I haven't seen.

Stumbled into the editing room at 9.30. Finished reel four then screened reel five with Camilla and discussed changes. Reel five has several big scenes in it, including the first swimming scene and the Tomato Fight. John continues to be tremendous, but I'm very pleased and relieved to see how strongly Sam is emerging. It's obvious when he loses his concentration, but when he's on, you can't take your eyes off him. His scene stealing the ceramic dwarf is priceless. He's called several times, asking how the film looks, wanting to get together. I've told him how excited I am with the film and his performance, but I find it difficult to make plans to see him. Or anyone for that matter.

I come home from the editing room, discuss my day with Jane over dinner. Shower, read for an hour, then go to bed. I can't wait to get back in the editing room. I am deeply imbedded in this film now. For the first time I feel connected to it on an instinctual level. I think of nothing else. It feels like every inch of film we shot, including every bad take, is stored in my brain like millions of megabytes of visual data on a gigantic hard disk and I keep sifting through it daily, hourly, in the middle of the night, trying to glean only the best moments. I like being this hermetic. I am also convinced that even the slightest deviation from this concentration will throw me off.

Had to rush to make my lunch meeting with Charlie Flax. To my surprise he was warm, gracious and quite intelligent. His conversation was sprinkled with lines he'd remembered from *Living in Oblivion*. I made a positive comment about his acting in general, taking care to avoid mentioning any films specifically, especially his last nine which I had not seen. The lunch ended, we said goodbye and I walked to the subway thinking, 'I just had lunch with Charlie Flax.' For some reason I had the strongest desire right then to curl up on the subway stairs and go to sleep for several hours.

THURSDAY 7 DECEMBER
Started working on the Opening Credits sequence. Looked at all the helicopter footage Paul Ryan and I shot in Knoxville. The

luscious green pastures dotted with thick rolls of hay, densely foliated trees all bathed in a clear yellow late-afternoon sunlight again reminded me of *The Wizard of Oz*. Something about the color, the sense of mystery, humor and magic evokes that film. *Box of Moonlight* is like a jeweled onion that keeps unfolding layer by layer.

Met Sam Rockwell for dinner at a cheap Japanese noodle bar on 49th Street. His finances made him very familiar with the place. We talked a lot about the movie, about our experiences working with each other. He said it was like having two fathers on the set, me and Turturro. At times he loved it, at times he hated me. It was strange sitting there hearing him say that. Part of me felt bad because I know I was pretty intense with him at times. Another part of me felt like wringing his neck. But, as I left, I was glad I'd agreed to meet him. Our friendship is still intact. I respect his honesty and I'm thrilled with what he does in the film.

FRIDAY 8 DECEMBER
Finished the opening credits sequence using Brian Eno's 'Spinning Away' as temp music. The music converged with stunning beauty with the images. We'll never be able to afford the rights to it, but it will give Egon Friske a sense of what I'm thinking and will work well for upcoming screenings.

We're supposed to have our first fine-cut screening on 6 January and we still have four reels to get through. Tom Rosenberg and Jonni Sigvahtsen from Lakeshore came by on Wednesday and I showed them three reels. It's the first they've seen of the film. They were very enthusiastic and had only one or two suggestions. I am somewhat astounded to find myself in this position of being paid to make a movie the way I want to make it, with a group of people who are actually very pleasant.

SATURDAY 16 DECEMBER
Cut big chunks out of two scenes today. I have a phobia about cutting stuff at this early stage. Due to pacing problems on *Johnny Suede* I had to cut so much that many of the transitions were destroyed and several scenes made no sense. I hate the feeling of trying to save a scene, to 'fake' it. It's hard to keep perspective on whether the reconstructed scene has any validity. At times like these I feel like a bad plastic surgeon, creating some half-living

creature with eyes and ears in the wrong places and gigantic stitches showing everywhere.

Egon Friske came by at five and we showed him four reels. He wanted to see more. I was pleased by his enthusiasm. He got very excited about the first driving sequence and wanted to redo the music I had selected there ('Wayward Nile' by the Chantays). I said I liked the original and he said he still wanted to redo it. Finally I told him no, that I had liked the Chantays piece for a long time and it was definitely going in. He then admitted the only reason he wanted to change it was because he also liked it and it made him want to do something like it himself.

I woke up in the middle of the night, remembering for some reason that when Egon had walked into the editing room, the first thing he'd done was take a quarter out of his pocket and flip it to the floor in front of me.

SATURDAY 23 DECEMBER

Strange how mental and emotional fluctuations synchronize with different sections of the film. Ever since Monday I've been struggling with a flood of despair about the film. Coincidentally, this whole week we've been imbedded in the film's darkest layers; the Wick/Kid antagonism, the mental abuse Al subjects his son Bobby to, the TV footage of Luvven Coddle's arrest for murder, ending finally in the brutal fight scene where Wick and Doob beat up Al and Kid.

All of this arouses my fear that these detours from the humor and sunny juvenile delinquency will throw the movie off balance. Nothing I can do about it; it's a theme that is deeply interwoven and impossible to remove even if I wanted to.

Worked on the Swimming Scene with Al, Kid, Floatie and Purlene. Laid 'Gomni', a piece of music by Ry Cooder and Ali Farka Toure, over the montage of everyone jumping off the rocks. It was astonishing to see how it married with the images. When it was over we replayed it; then again. The slow-motion images attach themselves irrevocably to the music; the bodies move in a rhythm and grace that seem almost balletic. Moments like this renew my astonishment at the power of music and image to act upon each other. Music videos have ground this magical power into Novocain.

Heard yesterday that Janet Maslin of the *New York Times* included *Living in Oblivion* on her Ten Best Films list. I received numerous calls from people offering their congratulations; all of them immediately asking, 'So, why doesn't the distributor rerelease it?' It's odd, but my first response upon seeing the mention was a sharp twinge of disappointment that the film's momentum was not better capitalized on. Every award or special mention the film gets only emphasizes my confusion as to why the film did not play longer.

I called the distributor and suggested that he rerelease the film. This idea was met with extremely cautious interest. I then enquired what the distributor's plans were in terms of the Academy Award nominations. He said he was living up to his commitment to seek a nomination for Best Original Screenplay by sending video cassettes to members of the Academy. I asked if he was taking out any ads in the trade papers, offering the film for the Academy's consideration. He said they planned to do that sometime in January, not wanting to 'overdo it' right away because the Academy members were too smart for that stuff and it tended to backfire.

I got off the phone feeling somewhat reassured that the distributor, as he'd insisted, was 'on top of things'. On my way home from the editing room, I stopped by a news-stand and thumbed through this week's *Variety*. I was about to put it back when something on the front cover caught my eye. It was a full-color advertisement for *The Brothers McMullen*, offering the film 'for your consideration' as Best Picture, Best Screenplay, Best Director, Best Actor and Best Actress.

I almost killed the legal-immigrant newsdealer who was scowling at me chanting, 'No buy megaseen; no look megaseen.'

My distributor took *Living in Oblivion*, admittedly a small film, and made it smaller (once I had to look at their newspaper ad with a magnifying glass just to see where the film was playing). The distributor of *The Brothers McMullen*, took a very small film, and made it enormous. The amount they spent is irrelevant. No matter what it cost, it worked. People saw the film. People are still seeing the film.

Jane and I had an early New Year's dinner at the Odeon. Each
table had gratis party hats laid out next to the silverware; silver
princess tiaras for the women and tiny dunce caps for the men.
Jane put her tiara on. At that moment I looked up and noticed
that at every table only the women were actually wearing their
party hats; all the men remained paper hatless.

Skip and Felicia, two recent actor friends of ours, dropped by
for a drink. Sometime during the evening, I placed a sharp
toothpick inside one of my Martini straws and blow-gunned it at a
nearby balloon, trying to pop it. It came close enough to inspire
me to keep trying. Felicia noticed and pointed at me in
amazement. 'Look at him!' she called out to Skip. 'Look what he's
doing! He's blowing toothpicks at balloons!'

'So what?' I said, expecting her to caution me about putting out
a waiter's eye.

'But you're a director!' Felicia exclaimed.

Is this the way most actors perceive the director: an emotional
blank, the dry, stern father who remains permanently hidden and
uncharacteristic behind the safe wall of control?

SATURDAY 6 JANUARY
Finished the first fine cut yesterday. Working with Camilla is a real
joy. She is tireless, absolutely committed and extremely patient
with me. We've developed a very intimate relationship. Jane calls
her my 'day wife'. I trust her eye and instinct implicitly and even
though I am meticulously involved in the cutting, I sense no ego
battles between us. Many times we'll be stuck on a certain cut and
I'll get up and go to the bathroom. Suddenly, while walking down
the corridor, an idea will strike me. I'll walk back into the editing
room and say, 'You know what, Camilla? What if we try . . . ?'
She'll look up from the table already in the midst of cutting in the
shot I had in mind.

TUESDAY 9 JANUARY
Went to see *Twelve Monkeys* over the weekend. Watching the
trailers before the film was like driving behind a garbage truck with
drunken garbage men hurling the refuse at your windshield with
all their might. Everything ends up in your face; the music, the
explosions, the gun shots, the quick cuts, the thudding

pronouncements of doom by the same asinine voice-over announcer. All is geared to grab you, to force you to pay attention. Perhaps next, distributors will send teams of Trailer-men into the theaters to accompany their movie trailers. During the trailers the Trailer-men will shoot real guns right next to people's ears, roll live hand-grenades under the seats, bang garbage can lids together an inch in front of viewers' noses, throw jars of hot paint against people's foreheads and hurl cinderblocks over the mezzanine balcony. The War Department ought to show trailers to troops just before they go into battle because after ten minutes I was screaming obscenities at the screen and would have killed my own dog in a second.

WEDNESDAY 10 JANUARY

8.30 p.m. Just stumbled home from the first fine-cut screening. With every film you forget what this first screening is like. After the lights come up you're so embarrassed at what you thought was an idea for a film that you wonder how you're even going to get out of your seat. You can't look in anyone's eyes because behind their murmured congratulations lies their undisguised panic at having just seen your film disintegrate. Yet you hang on every sentence, hoping someone will say the words that will make your own panic disappear forever. They never do. The words do not exist.

You know you're overreacting. You know you went through many fine cuts like this before the last film finally emerged. But still, you realize you should have never for one second considered yourself a film-maker. You realize that Tarantino is a genius after all and your only salvation is to immediately begin writing a script where guys in black suits shoot each other in their goatees.

And so, it starts all over again. What was on the page and in your mind must now be completely rediscovered with inch-wide strips of perforated plastic.

SATURDAY 13 JANUARY

Thankfully, the shock of the first fine cut wore off quicker than ones in the past. The general plan is clear; the film is there, it just needs to be much more tightly focused. Any information that is repeated has to come out. Turturro's performance is so strong that many of the character-revealing scenes I wrote are redundant. We get who he is immediately.

I made two very hefty cuts in some of John's scenes, several in Sam's and one very weighty one in Catherine's phone-sex scene as Varla. Anything that does not drive the story forward stops the film. Anything that draws attention to itself as 'meaningful' or 'significant' stops the film. What works best are the skittering, unremarked-upon moments and it is almost physically pleasurable to prune away all the dross that obscures them.

Some cuts were simple deletions; others involved extremely complicated reshaping and maneuvering around critical plot points and visual continuity in a scene. In two instances being able to make an important change affecting ten minutes of screen time depended entirely on forcing a single cut to work.

I called Catherine to tell her about the cuts I've made in her Varla scene. She took it well, but I know it hurts. The following morning Dermot left a message saying that *Living in Oblivion* had just been nominated for three Independent Spirit Awards: Best Picture, Best Screenplay and Best Supporting Actor – James Legros. To my great surprise neither Steve Buscemi or Catherine were nominated. I spoke to her again today and, although she bravely shrugged it off, she made reference to herself as the 'invisible' woman.

For some reason the American press has treated her as if she is indeed 'invisible'. My sense is that her performance is so effortlessly brilliant most people don't even see it. I am not alone in feeling this way; the Swedish Film Festival voted her Best Actress of 1995.

SUNDAY 14 JANUARY
Last week a white-owned clothing store in Harlem was fire-bombed by a black man who killed eight employees before killing himself. Yesterday, the FBI arrested six white men for plotting to blow up government buildings using the same type of fertilizer bomb that was used in Oklahoma City.

We are a nation blinded and paralysed by superstition and rage. Is it any wonder that our movie screens are full of explosions, disasters, exit wounds, sexy serial killers, English people in Victorian costumes and comedies about the dumbest people on earth?

Where does *Box of Moonlight* fit into this landscape? Will anyone see it? Will anyone give a shit if they don't?

Had another fine-cut screening Thursday. Invited a larger audience of people who had not seen the film. Asked Egon Friske to come, but he didn't show. Lakeshore's Executive Producer, Tom Rosenberg couldn't fly in due to the fog. Sat afterwards with my team and got some helpful suggestions. Came home and talked for an hour with Jim Mangold, the director of *Heavy*, who also had some good ideas.

In general, the notes echo my own belief that there is still more fat to come out. Came home and had a bleary message of apology from Egon Friske, who again did not show up. He has yet to see the entire film. We haven't even sat and talked about ideas. His carelessness and undisguised condescension are making me wonder if I made a mistake hiring him to do the music. I called and got his machine. It is now 10 p.m.; I have not heard from him since he agreed to show up at the 2 p.m. screening.

Spoke for a long time with Jim Jarmusch, who had been at the screening. He was surprisingly emotional about the film. He made specific comments on the acting and the story, which I really appreciated. I'm desperate to get a sense if people respond to what the film is about. It's amazing how many people are unable to speak about the film on an emotional level. One invited guest who urged me to call her afterwards because she had 'many important things to talk about', told me, 'The opening credits start over water then move to land. You can't start the film over water. Al is searching for water, you must start the opening helicopter shot over land.'

That was the 'important thing'.

I am fried.

TUESDAY 23 JANUARY
Started careful reel-by-reel fine-cutting on Monday. I am very excited about paring the film down to only what is necessary. The more I forget the script at this point the easier it is. I feel a little sheepish as to how much is actually coming out. Scenes and lines of dialogue I thought were crucial to the film now rise to the surface like sluggish chunks of debris.

In some cases I cut too much. Replacing three shots in Catherine's phone-sex scene suddenly gave it the arc it was missing. We're trying to finish two reels a day so we can show Cannes a completed film in April. Another screening has been set up for next Tuesday, the thirtieth.

SATURDAY 27 JANUARY
Worked on Saturday to try to catch up. Solved a problem with the flashbacks following the Fireworks Sequence that has been bugging me for a long time. I intercut them so that the two events happen simultaneously. Now, both reach a conclusion at the same time.

The idea of keeping things moving fascinates me. There is no reason the film has to stop just to explain something.

Came home and had a call from a local radio station in Utah that was interviewing directors who had previously been at the Sundance Film Fest. I expressed my opinion that Sundance has become the most important American festival; albeit the most troubling. What makes the festival so important is that it has become the launching pad for film-makers' careers. Every year the industry and media descend in hordes, rushing from film to film, from party to party in a frenzied, ferocious search for the next Soderbergh or Tarantino. The two times I've been there my genuine excitement has been marred by the desperate, near hysterical competition that this engenders in the film-makers. A distressing contradiction; all these talented people who have worked so hard, sacrificed and sold their own blood simply to get their film made, begin clawing for the prize worm like starving baby birds.

TUESDAY 30 JANUARY
Screening today at 2 p.m. Jane and I went down to the Magno screening room together. She had invited Mike Nichols, whose geniality put me at ease immediately. Turturro came with his agent, Bart Walker. Sam Rockwell came and Egon Friske finally showed up. A moment before the film started I took Turturro aside and forewarned him that since the film had been running long, I'd cut several lengthy scenes. He took the news calmly.

The film played well. Most of the changes we made worked; some of the cuts resulted in chopped-off moments so we will put them back. After the screening Sam Rockwell looked a little dazed. I think he's a bit stunned at what was cut. Turturro was initially reserved, but quickly warmed up. Knowing how I felt seeing the film for the first time, it is easy to understand both actors' reactions.

Mike Nichols was complimentary, but had to leave quickly because he was going to a fine-cut screening of his own film, *Birdcage*. Before he left he remarked how incredible Sam's performance was. Several people stated they had never seen Turturro this compelling, 'a whole different character for him'.

Went over to the editing room with Jane, Marcus, Camilla and Keiko and we talked about the next round of changes. The mood was up, I think everyone feels the shape of the film is there. The phone rang sometime later and it was Turturro calling to tell me how much he enjoyed the film. Sensing he was still feeling a little fragile after watching himself for almost two hours, I recounted several scenes for him, reminding him how the audience had responded so strongly. This appeared to reassure him and he was very supportive as we said goodbye.

Came home and had a call from Mike Nichols. He said what he appreciated most was that while the film was artful, there was nothing arty or pretentious about it. He said my work with Turturro had revealed John's true nature in a way that had not been seen before. Likewise he'd tried to do the same with Robin Williams in *Birdcage* and would be curious to see how audiences responded to him.

Had a call from Egon Friske. He apologized again for having missed the last two screenings and said he was very excited about starting work. I'm meeting him tomorrow at 4.30 to go over the film and spot for music. There is no question he's a talented composer. If he gives himself over to the film, the score could be incredible.

SUNDAY 4 FEBRUARY
Met with Egon Friske on Wednesday, Thursday and Friday after editing all day and spotted music from 6 to 10 p.m. He works closely with his arranger, calling out instruments, key and tempo changes while watching the film. The arranger writes them down, even sketching in the notes of the melody line. It's a different way of working for me. In the past I've been intimately involved in determining the tone and voicing of each cue.

Though I've known Egon for over ten years, I've never spent long periods of time working intimately with him. I think he sees that I have some knowledge of film and music. He plays me fragments on the guitar or synthesizer that approximate to what he is planning. It is a little disconcerting not to be able to hear the full idea with the image. The earliest I will be able to do this is at the rehearsal two weeks from now.

He played me a section of the Opening Credits that I wasn't wild about. It was tense and heavy. I told him I wanted the opening credits music to support the sense of flight and beauty the opening shot suggests. He said it would sound much better in the rehearsal. I cautioned him that the music should not become sour and reminded him of the goofy humor and magic in the film. Morricone came up as an example of emotional music that was also mysterious and playful. Friske had mentioned woodwinds and suddenly I thought of Prokofiev's *Peter and the Wolf*. Egon appeared very excited by the framework this provides him.

WEDNESDAY 14 FEBRUARY

Spent the last two nights down at Friske's, going through the film and listening to some more developed sketches he'd worked out. Several times I jumped out of my chair shouting 'Beautiful!' so loud some guy across the street cringed in embarrassment. Some cues, however, are still sounding more dour than I would like. One in particular, where Kid entices Al to go hunting with him, sounds like a droning dirge, suggesting all the joy of a bad acid trip. Friske got a little testy when I told him this. We argued some more about it until finally he said he would redo it.

His condescension is only part of what's annoying me. Friske has yet to have a conversation with me about the emotional thrust of the film. He's never said what he likes about the film; he's never said if it moves him in any way. Every time I try to speak to him about it on this level, he stares at me like a confused, sullen dog. I feel like I'm losing touch with this crucial element of the film.

Nevertheless, before I left for the night, I shook Friske's hand and told him, despite this one snag, I was very pleased with the music. He took my hand limply from where he lay on the couch and said, 'You're a hard one to read.'

I went home. The more I thought about it, the more odd this

43

statement became. I looked back at my behavior during the session and it seemed I'd expressed both my enthusiasm and my concerns very clearly. The only thing I could think of was that he was only hearing the criciticm and not the enthusiasm. So, I called him.

'Listen, Egon,' I said, 'I just want you to know that I think the music is sounding really beautiful. It's absolutely original and I think you're doing a great job.'

'Yeah, I am,' he said. 'And the music *is* sounding beautiful. But what you have to understand, man, is when I get these ideas, when this stuff comes to me it's like a Gift. It's my Gift and it's a Gift from me. And it's tough to just give it to you. It's really hard, man. It's hard.'

On the one hand, I appreciated his honesty. On the other, I found myself extremely close to yelling, 'Excuse me, shithead; you're not giving me this Gift for free; we're paying you a lot of money for it. In fact, if you cherish your Gift so much, and you're having such a hard time parting with it, maybe you should just stick it right back up your ass.'

I didn't say that. But just thinking it calmed me down enough to get about three hours' sleep.

SUNDAY 18 FEBRUARY
Spent the entire weekend writing looping lines for Turturro. He's coming into the sound studio on Tuesday to record these extra lines. This is the only chance to get him in before he leaves for Eastern Europe to shoot a film for six months.

Told Marcus some reservations I have about Friske. He said he knew it was difficult for me, but that he felt the music was sounding great. His advice was to try and get through it. The rehearsal with musicians is tomorrow. The actual recording session is scheduled for Wednesday and Thursday.

MONDAY 19 FEBRUARY
1.30 a.m. I just got home from the music rehearsal. It started out well, but ended in a grueling battle with Friske over the Opening Credits cue. The music did not sound better with real musicians; in fact it was even clearer that it is completely wrong for the film. It is heavy, tense and joyless. It cripples the opening shot. You can feel the images struggling to stay aloft and failing. I told Friske I was not happy with the cue. He ignored me.

44

Marcus came by at around 10 p.m. and I told him what was going on. We waited until after the musicians left and I told Friske I had real problems with the Opening Credits music. He got very upset. I got very upset. There was a lot of yelling and accusations and threatening to take names off movies before Friske finally agreed to try to reshape the Opening Credits cue slightly.

11.45 p.m.
Marcus called me a few minutes ago. He said he'd just spoken to Friske and was pleased to report he was still working on the new Opening Credits cue back at his apartment.

'That's great,' I said. 'But, I'm just curious, why isn't the Composer of this film talking to the Director of this film about how the music will be changed?'

A moment later, Marcus called back and said he'd told Friske I wanted to talk to him. Friske's response was, 'I don't want to talk to him.'

I argued with myself for a half an hour about whether I should call Friske or not. The conflict was between maintaining my dignity and choosing the most productive course of action for the film. Calling him would mean that he'd won, he had control, he'd forced me to come to him. Not calling him might make me feel better, but ultimately would only mean I could be as stubborn as he was.

This is an aspect of this business that I neither comprehend nor know how to deal with. Friske's attitude is abusive, hostile and blatantly destructive. He's acting this way because he knows he can; he's got something I need. He's playing power games with my score. Every bone in my body is urging me to go down to his apartment right now and beat the shit out of him, especially when I think of the years of frustration, poverty and emotional turmoil I went through just to get the movie made.

I called him. His machine picked up. I left a message thanking him for changing the Opening Credits cue.

TUESDAY 20 FEBRUARY
Slept about an hour. The whole night I kept hearing Friske's sour Opening Credits music. I was tense and exhausted when I met Turturro at the Looping Studio. He's lost about twenty pounds

45

for the film he's doing in Hungary, in which he plays a Holocaust survivor. I almost hugged him when I saw he wore his costume from *Box of Moonlight*; the white shirt, the blue pants and even the shoes. The pants were huge on him.

He was warm and very collaborative during the looping and the session went smoothly. I walked with him to the subway afterwards and we both made hesitant attempts to put what happened during the filming of *Box of Moonlight* into perspective. I think much of the tension between us came out of the fact we both felt the horrific schedule was keeping us from doing our best work. Bottom line though, he never gave up. Every moment of every take he dug in and tried to find something. I told him how rare that was in this business and how much I appreciated it.

We stopped on the corner of 27th and 7th. I was going uptown, he was going down. I contemplated suggesting we go have a drink right then; sit in a bar and clear the air. Instead, we stood on the corner and talked for a few more minutes about when he'd be coming back, would he be able to come to Cannes if we got accepted, then we embraced, he kissed me on the cheek and we separated.

FRIDAY 23 FEBRUARY
Finished recording the music this morning at 5 a.m. The first couple of hours in the studio on Wednesday were a little tense between Friske and I. We both were polite but careful. He resolved the Opening Credits issue by integrating a theme from another cue I liked. It's better than the original, but it still doesn't free the images the way I would have liked. However, once the cue was recorded, the tension eased somewhat. No mention was made of the argument two nights ago.

It was pretty exciting being in a studio with musicians playing live to sections of my film. The musicians Friske had gathered were excellent. Friske was great with them; relaxed, focused and concentrated. Occasionally, he would ask me if I liked a cue's placement, its tempo or the tone of a particular instrument. I stayed out of his way and only interjected when he seemed unsure about something.

His reworked version of the Hunting cue is very good; it has a hilarious tick-tocky playfulness that works well with the scene. The

Backwards cues (to cover all the scenes where Al sees things moving backwards) still seem too ominous and tense, with no magic or mystery. I might try to do these short Backwards Cues myself on the guitar.

Marcus called while we were recording. He's in LA to screen the film for Tom Rosenberg, the head of Lakeshore, and some of our foreign distributors. Sylvie l'Orange, the French distributor, wanted to see the film so she could advise us on the best way to approach screening it for Cannes. I was dismayed to hear Marcus say that while Sylvie liked the film she was convinced it would not do nearly as well in France as *Living in Oblivion*. She said the French like things that are either very funny or very serious and went on to explain this was why Jerry Lewis and Mickey Rourke are so popular there. She advised trying to get into the smaller Directors' Fortnight first, as opposed to any of Cannes' main competition sections.

A few minutes later, Rosenberg called me in the studio with some suggested cuts. One was very astute and I took him up on it. Another was about removing the jumping scene with Kid, Purlene and Floatie at the quarry. I told him it was one of my favorite sections of the film and with all due respect, I was leaving it in.

He asked me how the music was going. I said the music was going OK, but that Friske was proving to be kind of an asshole. His response was short and immediate: 'So, what do you hang around with assholes for?'

TUESDAY 27 FEBRUARY

Went through the entire film over the past three days and wrote fifteen pages of ADR (Additional Dialogue Recording) for scenes in which actors were off-camera or in the background, behind the main action. I did this for the lead actors as well as for extras who had non-speaking parts. When Al and Floatie talk on the rocks, I wrote a whole scene for Kid and Purlene who are off-camera in the water. I wrote them quickly with no revisions, almost like cinematic haiku.

The mother and her two children eating at the counter in the coffee shop where Al sees a cup of coffee pouring backwards:

FAT BOY: Mom, can I have a jelly donut?
MOM: No.

47

FAT BOY: Can I have a piece of banana cream pie?
MOM: No.
SIS: Mom, can I have Jackie's french fries?
MOM: Yes.
FAT BOY: Mom, can I have Candie's pickle?
MOM: No.

Most of it no one will hear. But I like the way it fills the backgrounds of peopled scenes with real chatter as opposed to the generic mumbling that usually gets laid in.

TUESDAY 5 MARCH

Sam Rockwell came into the looping studio today and did a whole day of looping. He was extremely precise in matching his lip movements for scenes where he had to replace problematic dialogue. We did have to pause for a while while he discovered I had cut one of his 'favorite' improvised lines. He moped around for several minutes, mourning out loud, until I somewhat energetically reminded him that I too had many 'favorite' things that did not end up in the film for one reason or another – including mistakes in my direction and, in some cases, mistakes in his acting. The rest of his looping went smoothly.

At 2 p.m. I went over to the music studio where Friske was mixing the music he'd recorded last week. He was in a good mood, having just finished mixing both Opening Credit versions. Upon hearing them both again, against the picture, I realized his original version had more interest and shape (primarily because it had been written to match specific visual changes). I told him then that was the cue we would use for the Opening Credits. He was happy to hear this. Although I made the right decision about the two cues, I still wish his version had more of the beauty and exhilaration evoked by the helicopter shot.

Spoke to Olivier Jahane, one of the programmers of the Director's Fortnight at Cannes. He and Henri de Leau will be in NY the week of 19 March. They will screen the film by themselves, along with a large number of other NY films. I wish we had a finished, mixed film to show them, but based on the strong reaction we've had with the work-print and temp music, I think we've got a chance. On the other hand, the reaction of our own French distributor starts a chill of dread in the pit of my stomach.

48

Spent the morning and afternoon in the looping studio, recording ADR for the extras. At 5 p.m. I went back over to the music studio to finish mixing the music with Friske. Again he was in a good mood. We laughed and joked frequently during the first three hours. Then suddenly, out of nowhere, a problem crept up. It seemed like a small one at first but in a matter of moments it escalated into a disaster.

The first phrase of the Opening Credits music was too long. Since the picture was locked and the cue could not be shortened, the only solution was to redo a shorter version of it. The only way to do this meant getting the musicians back, going back into the recording studio and rerecording it. Friske was unavailable and we did not have the money to do this.

As the scope of the problem increased, so did the tension in the room. Suddenly Friske snapped, 'It's not my fault!'

His defensive tone annoyed me, especially since nobody had been blaming anybody. I told him what we needed right now was to work together to solve the problem. What we didn't need was his attitude. I said this with a strenuous attempt to keep my voice calm and rational. Apparently, I did not succeed, because Friske suddenly exclaimed, 'Fuck you!'

And right then, the precious flower of our Director–Composer relationship blossomed into a thing of rare joy and beauty. I don't think I've ever used the word 'asshole' so frequently in so short a time.

As our collaboration reached its artistic conclusion, Friske turned and started to walk out of the room. I congratulated him for offering his exit as a creative solution to the problem. He stopped and sat down in silence. I paced the back of the room for several moments, also in silence. Finally Jim Flatto, my music editor, suggested we move on to another cue. The engineer forwarded the tape and slowly, quietly we started mixing the next cue.

Friske and I did not speak for the remainder of the night. At 1.30 a.m. we finished mixing the entire score with the exception of the 'problem' cue. The solution to that problem was left unresolved. I put my coat on, shook Friske's hand and thanked him for his work. He muttered something and I walked out.

Cut in Friske's score with Jim Flatto over the past two days. It's all being done digitally, which is a pretty amazing process. You can literally see the computer image of the music on the monitor and reshape it in a matter of seconds, all without a loss of tone or quality.

I've moved many of Friske's cues to spots they were not written for. As I suspected many of the cues still have a sour gloominess that completely deflates the film. I've isolated three or four of the more open and humorous cues and am attempting to intersperse them throughout the film. In some instances, I took single instrument hits from other cues and created new cues. Although the surgery appears to be working, I do realize this is an odd way to be manipulating the score; especially with only three days before the mix. Unfortunately, communication has completely broken down with Friske and it is impossible to ask him to redo anything. I have not heard a word from him in over a week.

TUESDAY 19 MARCH
Screened for the Director's Fortnight yesterday. The film was one of about 300 collected by the Independent Feature Project to be screened in succession at the Magno screening room. No one was permitted to attend except the two selectors, Olivier Jahane and his boss, Henri de Leau. The good news was (so the projectionist told us) that they sat all the way through it. No word as to their reaction.

Started the mix yesterday. It's going well; most of the ADR I wrote for the background actors adds a solid secondary layer to the film. Started with the dialogue tracks and hope to get halfway through the six reels by Wednesday when I'm going to LA for the Spirit Awards. The mixer is Dominic Tavella, who mixed both *Johnny Suede* and *Living in Oblivion*. He's smart, intuitive and fast; we're under tremendous pressure to finish the whole mix by 1 April. It's too bad we have to rush because I really enjoy this part of the process. The right sound can literally spark a scene into life. For the scene in Lyle's Garage, with Al, Kid and Wick, I wrote a fake race-car commercial and had a voice-over actor read it during the Group Looping session.

> Bring the whole family this 4th of July weekend to the Speedball Raceway! See stock cars! Funny cars! Customized dragsters! And kids! Don't forget to tell Dad to bring you down to

trackside to see the largest selection of semi-automated weaponry ever displayed legally in one state. AK-47s! M-38s! Chinese, jet-propelled grenade launchers! Genuine, US surface-to-air missile launchers! Plus a demonstration by State Militia Colonel Jim 'Paul Revere' Kaminsky on how you can build these awesome instruments of protection from kits in your own home! Fertilizer bombs! 35-gallon nerve gas recipes! All this Fourth of July weekend at the Speedball Raceway!

Put some schlock heavy metal over this and mixed it as if it were coming from a cheap, beat-up radio somewhere in the garage. It plays beneath the dialogue for the whole scene and adds a real layer of tension.

WEDNESDAY 20 MARCH
During a pause in the mixing this morning (we were in the middle of a very funny scene) I checked my machine and found I had a message from Olivier Jahane of the Director's Fortnight. I sensed immediately from the tone of his voice the news was not good. He left me a number to call him in Paris. I called and he got right to the point. He said de Leau did not respond to the film at all and there was no chance it would be accepted. I hung up, kicked the chair beside me so hard it went skidding across the mixing studio and crashed into a wall. Dom looked up in alarm and said, 'What's the matter?' I told him and walked out of the room.

It hurts; I can't deny it. Having spent five years writing and directing the film, it's hard not to take it personally. I'm also worried about Lakeshore's reaction. We all need a boost right now. The film is over budget and I've been forced to keep asking Lakeshore for more money. A positive response from the Director's Fortnight would have relieved a lot of anxiety. We still have two more chances; we screen for the Main Competition on 27 March, with a simultaneous option for consideration by Un Certain Regard. I seriously doubt we'll make the Main Competition, but there is a good chance we could get into the much smaller Un Certain Regard.

What if everyone says 'no'? There are already hints that I should prepare for this. The response in the US so far has been overwhelmingly positive. It may be that *Box of Moonlight* is an American film.

Writing this on the plane to LA. Jane and I are staying with
Catherine Keener and Dermot Mulroney for the weekend and
we're all going to the Spirit Awards together. I predict a sweep by
Leaving Las Vegas. The only thing *Living in Oblivion* has a shot at
is Best Original Screenplay, and *The Usual Suspects* will win that.

Finished the first three days of mixing yesterday. We start
mixing again on Monday and hopefully will get to the music by
the middle of the week. I'm going to sleep now.

FRIDAY 22 MARCH
Been in LA for two days. I always feel like I'm on another planet
when I'm here and am utterly amazed when I talk to people to
hear that they speak English.

One of my agents at William Morris threw a little party at his
house for the film. A small group of distributors, agents,
journalists and actors showed up. Out in the darkened patio I met
Andrei Konchalovsky. I told him how much I liked *Runaway
Train*. He informed me that he had been the president of the jury
at the Deauville Film Festival and his enthusiasm for *Living in
Oblivion* compelled him to urge the rest of the jury to award it Best
Picture. He analysed the film in such precise, minute detail it was
a little startling.

Jim Mangold came by later. He's in LA meeting actors like
Stallone and De Niro for his movie *Copland* which Miramax is
producing. He pulled me aside and pointed at the massive hill
rising steeply behind the house. I hadn't noticed it in the darkness,
but now I could see it gleaming faintly, completely covered in
sheets of enormous plastic spread out to keep any further
mudslides from washing the house away.

Have told no one about the Director's Fortnight rejection.

SATURDAY 23 MARCH
The Spirit Awards were held in a huge white tent set up in a
parking lot right off the beach in Santa Monica. The entrance was
lined on either side by a gauntlet of at least 150 journalists,
photographers and video crews. Dermot was recognized
immediately and fell behind with Catherine to accommodate the
press. Sandra Bullock was a few yards ahead of us. I was so
distracted by wondering which independent film she had done, I

walked right into her. Nicolas Cage was in front of her in a dense knot of photographers.

Inside, I ran into Tom Rothman, now head of Fox. Told him what a great job he'd done distributing *The Brothers McMullen*. He expressed his amazement and sympathies that *Living in Oblivion* had not done better. He left and I stood by our table for a while looking around me. I saw one or two people I knew; the rest were total strangers. It was rather unnerving. After twenty years in the independent film world, at the only ceremony honoring independent film, I felt I was at a real estate convention in Pasadena. Some acrobats came walking through on stilts, indicating it was time to begin the ceremony.

Samuel Jackson was the MC. He made a sincere effort to infuse an element of independent irreverence by dissing everything from Hollywood to Harvey Weinstein: 'Here's an award to everyone who's ever worked with Miramax and survived.' The irreverence – like the funk band and the idiots on stilts – seemed a little forced, as if everyone knew the whole deal was only the length of a limo away from emulating the Oscars and was kind of embarrassed about it.

Peter Bogdanovich gave a special award to Sam Fuller. He said the best advice he ever had was when Fuller said to him, 'If your first scene doesn't give you a hard-on, throw it out!' When the presentation was made to Fuller, the entire audience stood and applauded for over five minutes. Fuller remained seated and did not speak; his craggy face appeared on the monitors, dignified, overwhelmed and fighting back tears. I fought back tears myself seeing over two thousand people standing to honor this one man's life in film.

Best Supporting Actor went to Benicio del Toro in *The Usual Suspects*. Best Original Screenplay went to the guy who wrote *The Usual Suspects*. Any illusions I had about winning Best Picture were immediately put to rest when I saw the TV cameras moving into position in front of Mike Figgis's table a full minute before Sam Jackson announced, '*Leaving Las Vegas*'.

After the ceremony there was a long slow procession towards the exits. Trapped behind a tight knot of people taking meetings in the aisle, I glanced over and saw Sam Fuller and his wife, still seated, alone at their table. I went over and introduced myself. I told Sam one of my favorite moments in one of his films was in *Shock Corridor*. The journalist trapped in the mental institution stumbles upon a locked glass door. Looking inside he sees fifteen buxom women, pacing and panting in heat. Cut to his face as he registers alarm, then the word –

'Nymphos!' Fuller exclaimed, just before I did.

Instantly, in that brief exchange, my disappointment and frustration evaporated into the hot air rapidly filling the tent.

THURSDAY 28 MARCH

Back in NY on Monday. Crashed into the stress routine as if I'd never left.

8.30 on a cold, sleeting night. Screened *Box of Moonlight* yesterday afternoon in LA for Gilles Jacob, director of the Main Competition of the Cannes Film Festival. Jacob also selects for Un Certain Regard. Marcus stayed out in LA and arranged the screening for him. I am acutely aware that to expect a positive response borders on insanity. I have told myself to expect, and to accept the obvious: *Box of Moonlight* is not going to Cannes. This is not conjecture; it is fact. Nonetheless, every time the phone rings my heart leaps with the hope that it's Marcus calling with the Good News.

FRIDAY 29 MARCH

Got a call from Marcus in the mix today. He did not have the Good News. Jacob passed on the film for both the Main Competition and Un Certain Regard. It is now a fact: *Box of Moonlight* is not going to Cannes. I'm somewhat proud of myself for not kicking a chair this time.

SATURDAY 30 MARCH

Went to see *Fargo* this afternoon.

It is one of those amazingly simple pieces of work in which everything embellishes and supports everything else. There is no moral posturing, yet the film has a soul, epitomized with great skill and courage by Frances McDormand. The violence is shocking and macabre, yet one is always reminded the killers are crippled losers; not sexy philosophers in shades and black suits.

Worked on compiling more source music for the film over the weekend. I've had to replace half the music with less expensive songs due to the fact we are vastly over-budget for music. Nick Cave graciously gave me 'Red Right Hand' for practically nothing and I'll use it to replace Kool Moe Dee's 'Wild Wild West' which is unlicensable. Nick sent me a fax yesterday which consisted of a Thurber-like drawing of himself in his underwear watching *Living in Oblivion* on TV. He offered to work with me any time as either an actor or composer.

What a pleasure it would be to have an entire group of people – actors, crew, composers – with the same generosity and enthusiasm. Ultimately, I've realized when the film is over, the only lasting joy is in the doing; the chaotic interaction with collaborators dedicated to and united by the film. The bond created by this joint effort on the set is more thrilling and lasting than any good review or festival acceptance. In the face of a bad review and festival rejection, it is the only thing besides your will that helps you persevere. A crucial part of my job as a director is to be personally responsible for assembling this group.

I look at my experience with Friske with furor and terror. How could I not have not seen that hiring his talent also included his psychosis? What part of my willingness to believe the best of people is simply blind naïveté? No word from him at all.

TUESDAY 2 APRIL
Finished the first pass at the mix at one this afternoon. At five, we're taking the mix and the work print to a screening room as a final check to make sure it all sounds OK. We'll go back in the studio tomorrow and make final corrections.

We're only a day over schedule. I'm very pleased with what we've done, especially since we could have used another full week. The pace at which we've worked for the past ten days is like being on a coke jag. Dom has been a tremendous help; we make decisions on what stays, what goes, what needs to be louder, softer, sooner, later – all in a matter of seconds.

A large number of Friske's music cues have been either dropped or replaced with other cues. Eliza Paley (Supervising Sound Editor) and Paul Soucek (Effects Editor) have come up with an amazing palette of sound effects that in many instances work better than the music. Almost all of Kid's trailer scenes are laced with the off-screen sound of a woodpecker; its musical tapping is

55

both evocative and humorous. Insects, birds, wind, coyotes, distant trains, thunder, gunshots; it's all adding a dense, significant layer to the film.

WEDNESDAY 3 APRIL

It's funny how disaster can strike in an instant. Strolled into the final mix screening yesterday anticipating a few minor sound changes. From the first sour note of Friske's opening credits cue it was immediately clear the music is completely wrong for the film. It is dead, joyless and it anesthetizes the entire film.

The group meeting afterwards, originally intended to prioritize our notes for the final mix today, immediately disintegrated into panic as it became clear the music problem was enormous. The only relief I felt was hearing that the negative reaction to the music was unanimous. Dom said this kind of thing happens all the time and told me how on *Night on Earth*, Jim Jarmusch had to dump his entire score (composed by one of Japan's leading film composers) four days before the mix.

Whatever reassurance this story provided was quickly overwhelmed by the fact that in my case, the music has already been mixed, at considerable expense. What am I going to say when Lakeshore asks, 'Why did you spend all that money mixing the music if you didn't like it?' Despite my instincts to stop at every step of the way, I'd pushed on, trying to make it work out. Even in the mix I was changing cues, moving them; all with the hope that somehow a score could be salvaged that would justify how much we'd already paid Friske.

The whole thing is stunningly depressing, especially since I'd sensed the problem a month ago and met with such resistance from Friske when asking him to change it. My only choice is to start from scratch, respot the entire film, rerecord, remix; completely flushing Friske's fee and expenses down the drain.

I'm on my way to the editing room now to relisten to the score with Marcus and Camilla. We're going to see what, if anything, is useable. The scope of the catastrophe is so large I'm feeling the absurd impulse to burst into laughter.

2.25 p.m.

We had our meeting in the same mixing studio we've been mixing in. What had only yesterday been a warm and creatively intimate room now had the chilly gloom of a morgue. As an engineer went about setting up the mix for us to listen to, we started making a list of the cues that had some possibility of staying in. After a few minutes of this I stopped. Three things had become apparent: 1) even if we managed to save three or four cues there would still be giant holes in the score, 2) the general tone of Friske's entire score was too sour and leaden for the film and 3) given Friske's behavior, it would be impossible for me to have his name or a note of his music in the film.

In light of this, it appeared to me that relistening to the final mix was pointless. No one disagreed with me. Marcus will call Lakeshore and tell them we need to rescore the film. He has no idea how they'll take this news. My plan at this point, on both a practical and emotional level, is to offer the job to Jim Farmer. I should have done it months ago.

7 p.m.
Got out of the shower just as the phone rang. It was Marcus saying he'd just spoken to Tom Rosenberg from Lakeshore whose response to the news was not good. We conferenced Rosenberg. He said he didn't care if we changed the score. He trusted me enough that if I felt it should go, then we should change it. His only concern was who would pay for it. Lakeshore had already paid Friske a fee well over what had been originally budgeted for a composer. After a lengthy discussion we worked out a basic agreement in which Marcus and I would share the cost with Lakeshore. I would defer my final salary payment from *Box of Moonlight* as well as part of my fee on my next film *The Real Blonde*. I'm not entirely thrilled about spending money I don't have, but if it means purging the film of Friske's music I'll pay it all.

Called Jim Farmer and explained the situation. I felt very awkward and apologized repeatedly for not hiring him in the first place. He was extremely gracious and accepted the job immediately. I'll get him a tape of the film tomorrow and we'll spot the music on Saturday. He'll be able to start composing in about a week.

First day out of the cutting room and away from the film in over three months. Extremely disorienting, especially considering today was supposed to have been the day I finished the film. Spent most of the morning clearing off my desk, going through unanswered correspondence and throwing things away. Did a phone interview with someone from *Esquire* about *Box of Moonlight* and found it hard to complete a coherent sentence.

Even though I believe I did the right thing, a creepy sense of disaster has settled in. Everything has been put on hold. The film is incomplete, mired in a vague state of limbo and I am solely responsible. The only way out of it is to trudge through the debris and focus on the new score which will not be done until the end of May, almost two months from now.

What the hell is it with this film? Every step of the way has been accompanied by catastrophe, frustration and disappointment. It appears that if left alone the film would naturally gravitate towards its own demise. The only thing that has stopped it is my manic, desperate heavings and thrashings for the past five years. My task now is to try to shake off the onus of doom and failure. I have to see the film as continuing to be deserving of all my effort and hopes.

I'm starting to hate the film.

TUESDAY 9 APRIL
A bizarre day. Snowed heavily all day with no accumulation; the snow just melted into water immediately upon hitting the ground as if it was disappearing into the concrete.

Made a few calls. A British beer company is interested in me directing three commercials in Dublin. The spots are witty and well-written and I am seriously pursuing the job; a somewhat tricky feat due to the fact I'm steadfastly resisting it at the same time. However, given what looks like a pending hefty financial drain, I may need to take it.

Wrote a fake country pop song called, 'Gun Control', to use in *Box of Moonlight* as background music for the diner scene. I'm going to record it at home and do the vocals myself à la Merle Haggard.

> I'm a real American; Red, White and Blue.
> Born with the right to carry a gun
> And so my friend were you.

Paul Revere and Jefferson, John Wayne and the rest,
They all knew a loaded gun
Would serve America best.

But all those pansy Liberals, up in Washington,
They never faced a criminal
But they want to take our guns.

Gun Control, Gun Control, don't you tread on me.
Fill you full of bullet holes
You mess with my liberty.

WEDNESDAY 10 APRIL

Spent most of the day on the phone. One was a conference call
with the writers of the British beer ad. They've arranged to send
Byron, one of their writers, over from London tomorrow to meet
with me.

Rosenberg called and expressed his admiration and respect to
me for handling the Egon Friske issue without bringing in any of
'the assholes' by which he meant the lawyers and agents. Then we
spent forty-five minutes 'discussing' casting name actors in *The
Real Blonde*, which Lakeshore is producing.

I told him I had written Mary, the lead female part, for
Catherine Keener. In addition I have worked with her on three
films and my trust in her talent is unshakable. Rosenberg said he
wanted *The Real Blonde* to be a bigger film than *Box of Moonlight*,
with a higher profile and name actors so he could secure
distribution through a major studio. He said this film was very
important to him and he wanted to be actively involved in the
casting.

I said that likewise the film was very important to me. It seemed
to me we should determine immediately if what we felt was
important was, in fact, the same.

I hung up and it took me over an hour to calm down. It's not
that I don't understand his point of view. For the amount of
money he'll be spending he wants some guarantee the film will do
well at the box office. What distresses me is that progress in this
business appears synonymous with abandoning and ending all
relationships with friends and trusted collaborators. It appears that
the natural force in this business is an unrelenting tugging and

59

pulling away from anything you really want to do. Let's call it Maligma. Left unchecked, it will absorb everything in its path and shit it out in shiny, identical sugar-frosted turds.

Maligma is particularly insidious because it takes on any shape it needs in order to achieve its goal. The moment the first hint of financing appears, Maligma gallops up on a white charger waving the List like some holy banner of enlightenment. On this List are the Name Actors who will guarantee financing. Most of these Name Actors you have never seen in a film. The ones that you have seen are indistinguishable from the tree or wall they are hiding behind.

But these are the actors Maligma provides you with; for your film and every film about to be made. It is something akin to asking Mozart to write a lifetime of music – symphonies, operas, concertos – all to be played on the kazoo. And yet, you start to speak their names. You say things like, 'Well, what about Suzie A for the part of Mary?' And then you move on to Betty B because she's a little more hip, she's been in a couple of Preparation X films. And then Jenny C, and then Connie D, until suddenly you realize Maligma has been licking your ear all this time, whispering into it, 'Well Jenny C is not that great but if you cast her she'll bring x-number of ticket sales, she'll drive the foreign video market and then you'll get the six million to make the film.'

This is how powerful Maligma is. It creeps up on you quietly until the instant you realize it's there is the instant it has consumed you completely. There are two ways you can fight it. One, you can try to make it work for you. You say, 'In the real world no one is going to give me six million dollars and not expect a Name Actor.' The objective here is to take the six million and try to fool everybody into letting you make the best movie possible. You laugh, you sulk, you charm, you deal; you stride through offices and restaurants with determination. At every ethical crossroads you remind yourself, 'I am not being dishonest, I am not deceiving myself, I am not cheapening my vision. This is the real world here. Money is scarce, the competition is intense; this is what I have to do to make a six million-dollar film in the real world.' You Juggle, you Grin; you Play the Game.

Ultimately, this defense against Maligma is useless. It is based upon compromise and Maligma feeds on compromise. Because once you compromise then it is not *your* film, it is *Someone's.* It is not one person's vision, it is *Everyone's*: not too hard, not too soft, not too hot, not too cold, with a little pepperoni and some extra cheese.

The only viable way to prevent your film from turning to pizza is to fight Maligma with every ounce of your will, constantly, endlessly, without bitterness and without resentment. Fight to keep the script intact, fight to use the actors you want, fight to make the film for nothing after everyone turns you down. Then, just as you're feeling the most overwhelmed and hopeless, Maligma will tip-toe up and say, 'We really respect you for sticking to your guns. We want to make a six million-dollar film with you because of your bravery and commitment to truth. All we ask is that you put Jenny C in the lead.'

And finally you think maybe now would be a good time to accept this offer from Maligma. You ask some friends and trusted advisors for help with this decision. You say, 'God, I'm so tired of struggling and being broke and having ten people see my films. Maybe I should just cast Jenny C in this part and then move on to make a more "personal" film after this one. What do you think? I'm torn here; can you give me some advice?'

But the instant you ask for that advice Maligma slips in. Because no matter how trusted the advisor, the advice will always return to the fact that in the real world six million dollars is an awful lot of money. Now, that is not to say you will never get some advice from someone telling you, 'Yes, stick to your guns. Don't sell out. The movie is what matters. Tell that schmuck with six million dollars to fuck off!' In most cases, however, the person who gives you this advice either has nothing to lose, like your agent trying to impress you, or someone you just met on the subway, or another film-maker who's constantly getting money to do whatever they want.

The only one who can make this decision is you.

THURSDAY 11 APRIL
Marcus called this morning and said he was going to officially call Friske's agent and tell her we were dumping his score. I told him to have Friske call me as soon as he got the news so I could explain my decision personally.

Laid down the drum, bass and guitar for 'Gun Control' on my four-track until 11.30 a.m., when Byron from the British beer ad agency arrived from London. He proceeded to collapse on my couch and stare at me. I plunged into a fifteen-minute monologue about how excited I was about the job – at the end of which I suddenly realized that I didn't want to do a beer commercial in Dublin. Byron appeared to have arrived at a similar though unverbalized decision himself.

With nothing else to say, and wanting him to leave so I could finish 'Gun Control', I stood up and said I had to make some phone calls. I went into the kitchen and opened and closed the refrigerator a few times, hoping Byron would get the hint. When I returned to the living room he was still slouched on the couch. He asked if he could smoke. I said no. I said I had a lot of work to do. He said the ad agency had arranged for a car to pick him up at my apartment at 5.00 p.m. I looked at my watch. It was 12.30. He sat staring at me in dull confusion, apparently waiting for me to tell him he could stay on my couch for five hours. I said, 'Really great to meet you,' and walked toward the front door.

Finally he got up, picked up his coat and exited my apartment.

After messing with 'Gun Control' for a few hours, I went down to the editing room to check the opening titles with Sandra, the editing intern. She is the only member of the editing staff we can afford to employ now. She has been packing up the editing room for the last few days. It was depressing sitting at the editing table surrounded by stacks of sealed film boxes that will be put away for an indeterminate amount of time until we finish the score and ultimately finish the mix.

The titles, however, were exquisite. Michael Ventresco at the Effects house, designed a white typeface that appeared and grew slightly larger before fading out. This movement worked well with the sweeping flow of images we'd shot from the helicopter. It was such a relief seeing them without Friske's music, and even though I have no idea what Jim Farmer will replace it with, I feel a renewed hope for the sequence.

Just had a call from Marcus. He spoke to Friske and told him officially we were dumping the score. I asked Marcus what Friske's reaction was to this news. He said Friske seemed somewhat dumbfounded and kept asking if we were dumping the entire score. Marcus said he asked Friske if he was going to call me and Friske said no.

His refusal to speak with me only confirms my opinion of him. We have not spoken since 6 March, over a month ago.

SATURDAY 13 APRIL

Finished spotting the music with Jim Farmer. We discussed instrumentation and mood at length. I told him that at no time should the music be solely one thing. If it was an emotional cue then the music should be hyper-emotional, edging into satire. I said it should be rich, open and always imbued with a hint of magic and humor. He's going to use a palette of specifically American sounds: fingersnaps, Jew's harp, electric guitar with whammy bar, harmonica, acoustic bass and banjo. He said he would start with the smaller cues first, leaving the Opening and Closing credits for last after the texture of the score had been more defined. I left his studio feeling very excited.

The more I think about what has happened, the more I realize it is for the best. In fact, on some level, I was probably aware that it was necessary for me to bring the film to a complete halt. That is the one thing low-budget film-makers fear the most; that all forward momentum of the film, created only after years of super-human effort, will come to a stop. The customary procedure is to continue at all costs. Lose an actor before shooting, recast over the weekend and keep on schedule. Lose a location during shooting, find a replacement or rewrite the scene; anything to keep moving. A stalled film is a dead film.

Yet once you get past that horror and actually start walking around in the dreaded stasis, it's not so frightening. In fact, I feel more clear about the film than I have for several months. Particularly with the music, I had lost my perspective. I had been so crazed with trying to finish the film, writing the ADR, recording it with the actors, trying to find source music we could afford, recutting at the last minute – I couldn't see until the mix that Friske's score was absolutely wrong. I feel fortunate that I saw it at all.

TUESDAY 16 APRIL

Met with Bart Walker from ICM at 11 a.m. He stressed again ICM's interest in signing me. He spoke intently about his work arranging financing for independent film-makers including Jarmusch, Tim Robbins, Mike Figgis, Mira Nair and Ed Burns. All of whom have final cut; all of whom own their own films. I decided I would let Bart represent me.

Came home and called my agents to tell them I was leaving William Morris. They both expressed their shock and immediately wanted to know what they had done wrong. I told them they had done nothing wrong and in fact I liked and respected them both very much. I said I preferred not to get into the 'whys' and asked them to respect my decision as being what I felt was best for me.

They wanted to fly to NY and talk to me. I said no. They said they were coming anyway. I said the decision was final. They both kept asking what they had done wrong. I was not quite prepared for the responsibility of their distress and hurt feelings. Unfortunately, the more I expressed my sympathy and my own distress, the more they insisted on flying in to talk to me. Finally, I realized there was no happy way to end this and I would have to take on the unpleasant task of being the one to say it's over. I did.

MONDAY 22 APRIL

Met with Jim Farmer yesterday and he played me the first eight cues he'd written for the film. All of them were exquisite. The theme he's created for the backwards images is beautiful, mysterious and emotional all at the same time. It works particularly well over the shots of Al staring in astonishment; it brings out a deep rush of feeling for him. Friske's music was like a wall here, closing Al off.

On the simplest level, working with Jim is infinitely more enjoyable and creative. He is open to my suggestions and he doesn't take it personally if I ask him to change the voicing of a phrase. There is a sense of play between us that allows the musical ideas to emerge as instinctively as taking a breath.

TUESDAY 23 APRIL

Flew to Chicago with Marcus to meet with Rosenberg about casting on *The Real Blonde*. Met for lunch in the hotel's 39th-floor dining-room. The room was lined with glass on two sides and more than once I found myself staring past Rosenberg's head at Lake Michigan; white-capped and dark blue in the distance. We wrestled with casting ideas for over three hours.

'What's with this Mary list?' he asked. 'There's only three names on it.'

'Yeah, I know,' I said, 'and that's two too many.'

He laughed, although I know he did not think it was funny.

'Listen, Tom,' I said. 'I've worked with Catherine Keener on all three of my films and what I know about her as an actress convinces me without a doubt she is the one.'

'I don't understand why you're being so rigid about this,' he said. 'What about Nicole Kidman, Uma Thurman or Tea Leoni?'

'None of them would meet me without an offer. I don't think it's fair to expect me to just hand the part over to someone I don't know.'

We ended the round about even and moved on to the list of Joes. As I predicted, it was painfully small. Johnny Depp is on it; Matthew Modine and Kevin Bacon were discussed as well as Steve Buscemi.

'I'll tell you this right now,' Rosenberg said, 'I'm not making this film with Keener *and* Buscemi.'

I wasn't looking at him when he said this; I was staring at the waves breaking on the tiny, lone jetty about four miles out on the lake. Rosenberg did surprise me with some astute casting choices, though. He knows his movies and he has a clear sense of who is and isn't a strong actor. We ended the meeting agreeing that casting Joe was our biggest hurdle. The plan is to hire a casting dirctor as soon as possible. The issue of Mary was left unresolved.

Seeing the look of distress on my face, he laughed and hugged me as I was leaving.

'Look at this guy,' he said. 'He's fighting me, he's killing me with this Catherine Keener thing!'

'Yep,' I said, 'it's the age-old battle between Art and Commerce.'

'Yeah,' he laughed again, 'and I'm the Art!'

Had one beer on the plane and immediately fell asleep.

FRIDAY 26 APRIL
Saw two interesting headlines on the subway down to Jim Farmer's yesterday:

TOKYO GAS GURU SAYS AIM WAS TO GIVE 'ULTIMATE JOY'

MATHEMATICIANS SAY ASTEROID MAY HIT EARTH IN A MILLION
YEARS

The first prompts me to think very hard about Ultimate Joy, what it is and where to find it. The second prompts me to think very hard that these mathematicians have been smoking it.

If indeed the earth is still here in a million years, I seriously doubt if an approaching asteroid will divert the world's attention from the wedding of Madonna's great-great-great-great-great granddaughter and Michael Jackson's head (both preserved in liquid nitrogen).

THURSDAY 2 MAY
Interviewed four casting directors yesterday for *The Real Blonde*. Amazingly, all four came into the meetings and said unsolicited how perfect Catherine Keener would be for the role of Mary. Decided to go with Avy Kaufman; simple, clear, direct, very experienced, great credits and I liked her.

This unanimous observation about Catherine has prompted this decision: I will not make *The Real Blonde* without her. It is morally, ethically and artistically wrong. My hope is that Tom Rosenberg sees how passionately I believe she is right for the part, and agrees to cast her. It has become an extremely personal issue for me. If ascending into the rarefied air of Success means scraping away anything meaningful, discarding all relationships, friends and collaborators who helped you get there, what part of me is being scraped away also?

I know this much about myself: I cannot make a movie without engaging in a deep, resonant bond with those helping me make it. I've seen miraculous creative achievements develop from this bond. And in this world of smirking, hip idiocy, that bond is a rare thing. At times I'm probably too desperate in my yearning for it. I know at times I require that bond of intimacy to keep me from the feeling I'm alone and drowning in a gigantic sea of shit.

SATURDAY 4 MAY
Spent the afternoon with Jim Farmer listening to his latest batch of music cues for *Box of Moonlight*. He's making great progress; his music has a lush, whimsical beauty that brings out both the humor

and the emotion of the film. In the scene at Splatchee Lake where Reverend Luvven Coddle comforts Al, I asked Jim to have the music literally caress Al with poignant, angelic sweetness. Jim's music, a lilting whisper with plucked harp, strings and choir, does an amazing thing. It emotionalizes Al's sense of loss and yearning but at the same time makes Luvven Coddle absolutely hilarious. I told Jim this cue should guide us in all the rest of the music and always have this duality.

I brought down my tape of 'Gun Control' and we transferred it to Jim's twenty-four-track digital record. We'll mess around with it next week and see if it needs anything added on other tracks. This creative goofiness would have been impossible with Egon Friske.

It is such a relief to finally see the music slipping into reality. Unfortunately, the final remix is still an interminable month away. We've got three days scheduled with Dominic Tavella starting 3 June.

SUNDAY 5 MAY

Ran into Miramax's Harvey Weinstein at the *Dead Man* première. He asked me if I was interested in rereleasing a director's cut of *Johnny Suede*, since 'this Pitt kid is the hottest thing in America'.

I was a little confused, considering my Director's Cut was the version Miramax released for two weeks five years ago. I chose not to mention this, and asked him instead if he was seriously interested in rereleasing the film.

'Absolutely serious. Absolutely interested. Call me Monday.'

I've often thought about recutting the film since its disappointing release. I do have some ideas about how to pick up the pace and reinstate several lost scenes. However, returning to the film after all this time feels a little macabre, like opening a crypt.

TUESDAY 7 MAY

No response yesterday and none today from Miramax regarding the *Johnny Suede* issue. Everyone leaves tomorrow for Cannes. I'm sure this absolutely serious issue is absolutely dead.

MONDAY 20 MAY

Met Matthew Modine on Friday. I'd asked him to read *The Real*

Blonde and look at the part of Joe. He read it and agreed to meet with me without an offer. He was perceptive, gracious and openly enthusiastic about his interest in the part. I took a liking to him immediately. We offered him the part today. He accepted.

It's a little startling how quickly it happened. In contrast, it took me three months to get Turturro to read *Box of Moonlight*, another two to arrange a meeting, and another year before he agreed to play the part of Al.

Went down to Jim Farmer's studio on Sunday to listen to the final series of music cues. They are all beautiful and only need minor adjustments. This is impressive considering the major setback Jim had two nights ago. He'd opted to go 'hogwild' in the celebration of his birthday and combined Ecstasy with several bottles of champagne. He was still cross-eyed when I saw him yesterday.

He'd written a bouncy, hillbilly piece with banjo for the Tomato Fight which worked well, but seemed a little too 'country'. Last week I'd suggested leaving everything the same but adding a hip-hop beat and bass line. What he played for me yesterday was hilarious. He'd put rap scratches, barking dogs, a hip-hop beat and a very fat bass line under the plinking banjo. I do believe it is the first fusion of hip-hop and hillbilly in the history of recorded music.

The only cues he's got left to do are the biggest: the Opening and Closing Credits. We're both feeling the crunch a little bit; everything has to be done by the 28th when I cut the music in with Eliza Paley. Just before I left, Jim threw his hands on the keyboard and tapped out a little riff in his frustration.

'What was that?' I asked.

'What?' Jim replied.

'What you just played.'

'This?' He played it again.

I started whistling and snapping my fingers and the next thing I knew he'd developed the riff into a beautifully simple melody with a groove. We decided right then this would be the basis for both the Opening Credits and the Jumping Cue – the montage where Kid, Floatie and Purlene jump off the rocks into the water. It makes sense thematically for these cues to be the same; both are about release and the joy of flight.

I can't wait to hear how he develops it. I really think we've got it.

SUNDAY 26 MAY

I was lying on the couch doing nothing last night when Mike Nichols called. He wanted to know if we had a distributor for *Box of Moonlight* yet. I told him we didn't, but that we were setting up a screening next month for distributors in LA. He gave me a contact at United Artists and told me to call him Monday.

I felt considerably tongue-tied in the face of such generosity and actually heard myself say, 'So listen, Mike, if there's anything I can ever do for you, just let me know.'

MONDAY 27 MAY

Called the contact at UA. He said he'd already spoken to Mike Nichols and would definitely come to the LA screening next month.

Went down to Jim Farmer's and he played me the Opening Credits music. It is stunning. It has everything I've ever imagined for this crucial, three-minute piece of film: beauty, humor, mystery, joy and a hint of magic. I knew with the right music these images would soar and finally they do. I embraced Jim, practically in tears. He gave me the DAT tapes of the entire score and I left.

As I rode the subway home, I kept gripping the tapes tighter, as if they were somehow going to fall out of my hands and end up under the wheels of the train. They were the final elements of a film that had taken me over five years to complete. No matter what happens to it now, at last I can say this is the film I wanted to make. At last there is nothing I feel the need to apologize for. Suddenly, I felt a flood of peace and relief wash over me like a balm.

WEDNESDAY 5 JUNE

Finished the music remix today at 3.00 p.m. The new music cut in so effortlessly we were also able to do some tweaking on the dialogue and effects tracks. The film is done. We screen on the twentieth for US distributors. I expressed my belief that we should wait for the support of a major festival. Lakeshore vetoed this, since the nearest one is Toronto, at the beginning of September. We've already got an official invitation to Locarno at the end of August. Many distributors had been expecting to see the film two months ago, before the Egon Friske fiasco occurred. Rosenberg is concerned that they will think there is something wrong with the film if we delay again.

THURSDAY 20 JUNE

Arrived in LA yesterday. To accommodate both east and west coast distributors, we decided to have two simultaneous screenings; one in NYC and one in LA. Since I was in LA to begin casting for *The Real Blonde*, I attended that screening tonight.

A half hour before the screening, Marcus and I were sitting outside, downing double espressos at a coffee bar in Santa Monica. Marcus's cell phone rang and it was Bart Walker calling from NY to tell us the screening there was phenomenal. He said they had to turn people away and there was laughter from beginning to end. He couldn't talk long because he was on his way to a meeting with Christy Fletchor and Mickey Winkling, Acquisition Execs from Miramax who were 'wild' about the film. Before hanging up, Bart stated he felt sure we'd have at least four or five offers.

Buoyed by this news, I went into the LA screening with a renewed confidence about the film. Afterwards, the response from people echoed my own; the film is strange, beautiful, funny and deeply moving. Again, people's reactions were sharply divided between those who marveled at Turturro and those who loved Sam Rockwell. Everyone raved about the music.

Went back to the hotel and had two messages. One was from a young man to his girlfriend, who unbeknown to him, had checked out. His voice was sweet, sincere and full of uncensored love. He hoped she was doing well 'out there in LA' and urged her to come home soon so he could do to her left foot what he had started doing to her right the night before she left.

The second message was for me, from Christy Fletchor and Mickey Winkling. Christy spoke at length about how much she and Mickey loved the film, the look, the acting, Turturro, Sam Rockwell, its comment on America. Mickey interjected from time to time with his own congratulations, thanking me for portraying a mid-life crisis that so deeply echoed and gave meaning to his own. They both urged me to please give Miramax strong consideration as the best distributor for the film. They said this would be a perfect chance for Miramax to mend fences with me and hopefully assuage any disappointment I might still have over their release of *Johnny Suede*.

FRIDAY 21 JUNE

Spent all day casting, with breaks every twenty minutes to track the distributors' responses. Despite our intent to have all the distributors come to the two screenings, some are calling now to set up private screenings for their upper executives. Alarmingly, some of my preferred distributors never even showed up.

The heads of Miramax saw the film today. The response was strong enough for them to make an offer to Rosenberg. I was dumbfounded to hear how low the offer was. As pleased as I am in their interest and their desire to 'mend the fences' with me, I cautioned Rosenberg to pursue other offers. He assured me he was and told me he'd already informed Miramax that he couldn't accept such a low offer.

We are all feeling very uneasy. All the other distributors appear to be running away. At the moment there has been no word from Sony Classics. October seems about to pass. No one from Gramercy went to see the film. No word if they want to see it now. No word from Fine Line. UA has passed, the contact secretly informing me that their company is about to be sold.

Fox/Searchlight has passed. The new company head is not interested in seeing the film based upon the negative report he received from his Acquisition team who attended the LA screening. Marcus is particularly disturbed by Searchlight's response. The company head is a friend of his, for whom he produced six films in the past.

MONDAY 24 JUNE

Miramax has held firm and declined to raise its offer.

All the other independent distributors have now officially passed.

On the phone, Bart Walker said he was stunned by their response. I asked if there was any chance Miramax might pull out of its offer. Bart said that was impossible. In his conversation with them this morning, Miramax had assured him they were buying the film.

'Besides,' Bart went on, 'they really want to do business with you. They're not going to jeopardize their reputation or their future relationship with you.'

Had another phone call from Christy Fletchor and Mickey

Winkling which ended with the unsettling. 'No matter what happens we just want you to know we still really love your film.'

Rosenberg called the hotel this morning, waking me up. He said Miramax had withdrawn their offer.

'An interesting way to mend fences,' I said.

'I fought them,' Rosenberg replied, 'I brought all my lawyers in and finally decided it was better to let them wriggle out. I'd rather have the film with a distributor who wants it instead of winning a lawsuit.'

He said Miramax obviously felt embarrassed because they sent him a bouquet of flowers.

'Flowers? What kind of flowers?' I asked.

'I don't know; carnations, gladioli,' Rosenberg said. 'With a note saying, "We owe you one; you have our word on this."'

'Was the note printed on toilet paper?'

Rosenberg cautioned me from taking any of it personally, and to my great relief and amazement, he went on to reiterate his faith in the film – an extremely gracious action from an Executive Producer in the face of this unanimous cold shoulder from the distributors. In addition, Rosenberg said he was more than happy to hold out and run the Festival route. A lone bit of good news came this morning; the film was officially invited to the Toronto Film Festival in September. A strong audience and critical reaction there and at Locarno could rekindle interest in the film.

WEDNESDAY 26 JUNE
Back in NY this morning. I keep expecting the phone to ring and to hear someone laugh, telling me the whole thing is a joke. Never, in my worst fits of anxiety did I expect a response as devastating as this. Every single distributor has passed; it is difficult not to take it personally. I am paralysed by equal amounts of rage and fear.

It appears that no distributor sees 'money' in the film. Yet, everyone who's seen it appears deeply moved by it. In the mail today, I got three letters from people at both the NY and LA screenings, expressing their delight and strong emotional response.

It is particularly frightening to think that five years of such intense, passionate labor should result in a product that is deemed worthless.

Urgent phone call from Marcus tonight at 7.30. Both the Locarno
and Venice Film Festivals have expressed interest in the film.
Festival regulations make it impossible to go to both. Locarno has
officially invited us and wants to give us maximum exposure in the
main competition, with a prestige screening in their outdoor
piazza with an audience of 7,000.

Venice, on the other hand, cannot guarantee a main
competition slot, but is offering an invitation to a smaller sidebar
called the Fast Track. Flauto Prescelloni, our festival contact at
Locarno, scoffed when I told him this.

'The Fast Track is merely the garbage bin of the Main
Competition,' he stated. 'The films are shown in horrible theaters
and no one goes to see them.' He went on to insist that he needed
an answer from me today.

After several hours of phone calls, we managed to squeeze
another forty-eight hours out of Locarno. I promised Marco
Mueller, the Festival Director and a strong supporter since *Johnny
Suede* won in 1991, that we would not accept a sidebar invitation
from Venice. If by Wednesday they have not offered us a Main
Competition slot, we would accept his invitation and go to Locarno.

TUESDAY 2 JULY
Spent most of the day on the phone. After numerous calls to
Venice we could only get a reiteration of their invitation to their
sidebar, out of competition. They did say, however, that Gillo
Pontecorvo had seen the film and was not ruling it out for the
main competition.

After several hours of deliberation with Marcus and Tom
Rosenberg, we decided to take the chance and pass on Locarno.
Called Flauto Prescelloni and told him the news. He was very
unhappy – to the point of belligerence. Upon hearing that we'd
made our decision based upon the information that Pontecorvo
might consider the film for the Main Competition, Flauto sniffed
loudly into the phone. 'If you think Pontecorvo is going to change
his mind then you must still believe in Santa Claus!'

Later spoke to Marco Mueller directly and expressed my
disappointment about passing on his invitation. He was courteous
but cool and also intimated we'd made a bad decision.

FRIDAY 19 JULY

Still no word from Venice on the Main Competition. They have assured us, though, that no matter what, we have an invitation to the Fast Track. To maximize the presence at Venice in either capacity, Largo (our foreign sales company) has hired Simona Benzakein to do publicity at the Festival.

She has attempted to get a more definitive answer from Pontecorvo to no avail. It appears that there are several other American films they are considering, all in various stages of completion. We've been hearing 'the day after tomorrow' for two weeks.

TUESDAY 6 AUGUST

Came home from a production meeting on *The Real Blonde* and found a message from Simona Benzakein. She told me she had just spoken to Gillo Pontecorvo and he had accepted *Box of Moonlight* into the Main Competition at Venice. I was alone in the apartment and it seemed like a good time to scream out loud.

SATURDAY 10 AUGUST 1996

One year ago I flew down to Knoxville to begin pre-production on *Box of Moonlight*. Next week I begin pre-production on *The Real Blonde*. Rosenberg has finally agreed to cast Catherine Keener.

I am going to end this diary for a while.

epilogue

MONDAY 9 SEPTEMBER 1996
Flew into Venice in the early morning. Rising sun gleaming over
marshes, lagoons and winding canals; domed churches and spires
of antiquity standing beside towering smokestacks and exhaust
towers of oil refineries.

Met Simona Benzakein on the terrace of the Excelsior Hotel on
the Lido. A brilliant blue sky, intense sun, the sea blinding white
just beyond the wedding-cake balconies and staircases of the hotel.
All the publicity for the festival takes place here. Every few feet
someone was being interviewed by video crews poised at attention
and photographers jostling for position just out of camera range.

A blonde Italian movie star behind us was surrounded by
paparazzi yelling, 'Deborah! Deborah! *Per favore, anche per io!*'
Gina Gershon, co-star of *Bound*, stood posing for photographers
in front of a pink cabana. She pursed her lips, turned her eyes
skyward and glared sternly at a small cloud hanging innocently
overhead.

Roman Polanski suddenly emerged from the pool, wearing tiny
black trunks. He had a slight paunch and looked somewhat like a
vacationing leprechaun. He's on the jury, along with Angelica
Huston and Paul Auster.

Started the next day with a press conference at 11 a.m. Simona
told me the film had been well received at the Press Screening the
day before and most of the questions were supportive and
perceptive. Someone wanted to know if I was a member of
Greenpeace. Someone else wanted to know how long I had been a
student of American Indian culture and seemed a little
disappointed when I revealed that all the Indian lore Kid spouts in
the film is complete gibberish.

Suddenly an older woman stood up and announced in a
particularly distraught voice, 'I'm sorry. I watched the film
yesterday and heard everyone laughing and I didn't understand
one thing they were laughing at. I did not get your film at all. I see
now you are not a simpleton, but instead a fairly clear-minded

person, so I am wondering could you please tell me what I missed in your film?'

It was a little unnerving hearing her say this in front of over a hundred journalists, but I told her without any sarcasm or ridicule that it was alright if she didn't get the film and the main thing was for her not to feel bad about it. She stared at me in confusion for a moment then sat quickly as the room suddenly filled with applause.

An 'official' photo session immediately after. Led out on to a balcony where sixty photographers waited, standing in tight rows on tiered platforms. A chair on a small stage awaited me. I sat down and was immediately met by a barrage of yelling.

'DiCillo! DiCillo! Look here, DiCillo! Tom! This way, Tom! And another! DiCillo!'

In amazement I took out my camera and took a picture of the photographers. They were completely unfazed and only yelled louder and faster, 'Lower the camera, Tom! Good! Just a little higher with the camera, DiCillo! Like that! And one more for me, DiCillo – look here!'

The Main Competition screening was at 6.30. Our group assembled by the swimming pool in the rear of the hotel where we were met by our Festival Hostesses. These were two young Italian women, both with long, dark hair and both wearing slinky black sheath dresses and high heels. They directed us to an old gate behind the hotel and suddenly we were on the street in front of the theater. A red carpet ran across the street and into the crowded theater entrance.

Now I saw what the Hostesses were for. They led the procession, setting the pace, sashaying slowly in front of us like young mares in a Thanksgiving Day parade. Photographers and video crews waiting behind aluminum railings, started shooting as we approached. A woman thrust a microphone in front of me and yelled, 'Ah, Tom – so here you are at the Venice Film Festival. Can you tell us now what is the meaning of your title, *Boxing Moonlight*?' The answer I gave was such stuttered nonsense that even I didn't understand it. I suddenly realized the lilting music that was coming from a row of loud speakers and echoing along the street was Jim Farmer's opening credit music.

76

Gillo Pontecorvo appeared beside me. Without taking his eyes off the swaying butts of the Hostesses in front of us he leaned close and whispered, 'Turturro must come. I cannot guarantee it, but I think he will win Best Actor. You must call him!'

Then we were inside the theater. Simona led us to our seats high up in the balcony. Looking down at the 1500 people spread out below me prompted the sweat to start trickling down my ribcage. The lights went down and the film started. Practically no laughter for the first twenty minutes. Then suddenly, after Kid pushes the cop car down the hill, a sharp burst of applause.

There was more applause when Turturro stood up and started dancing, but the mood had quieted again by the time the film ended. As the closing credits began I felt the horrible dread begin; anticipation of faint, polite applause dying out quickly, me rising from my seat with a hard, frozen smile on my face, trying hard to conceal my disappointment.

The applause began and to my astonishment, continued; grew louder. In disbelief I watched as people stood; I thought they were getting up to leave. Instead the entire audience rose, turned to where I was sitting and continued to applaud. I suddenly heard Simona's voice yelling from my left, 'Stand up, you idiot!'

77

I stood and the applause swelled from the sea of faces fixed on me. I turned to look at Jane to keep myself from bursting into tears. I had to look away quickly; she was crying, smiling at me. I urged Marcus to stand, then Camilla and then Jim Farmer. Glancing behind me I saw the whole theater was on their feet, beaming at us in delight. I felt like I was flying. I finally took off my jacket and saw my shirt was as wet as if someone had thrown a bucket of water on me.

Simona led us out into the lobby. Teenagers stuck autograph books at me. An older couple rushed up, the man yelling, 'Thank you, DiCillo, for this *Box of Moonlight*!' Out on to the street, more autographs, more yelling. Ran back to the Excelsior and found a phone. Called Turturro in NYC. Left a message on his machine telling him what had happened and relaying Pontecorvo's whispered plea to me. I hung up and headed down a long corridor leading to the wharf where Jane and the rest of our group were waiting. Just then Julian Schnabel's boat arrived. Schnabel's film *Basquiat* is also in the Main Competition. About thirty photographers and journalists swarmed around his boat, then roiled back as Schnabel got out and marched, plump, bearded and swaggering down the corridor toward me.

I stepped aside to let his procession pass. They continued down the hall and ascended the stairs that lead to the main lobby. Staring after them from the now-deserted corridor, I suddenly saw the wall and ceiling above the staircase blossom into a continuous stutter of blue-white flashes from another group of photographers waiting for Schnabel in the lobby.

The precious jewel of my own triumph only a half-hour before, crumbled into dust so quickly it left me stunned and gasping like a junkie for his next fix. Fame is the purest dope there is. One hit and you're addicted. A moment later it's gone and instantly you need another.

Simona woke me at 9 a.m. to finish the last day of press. Had to stand in an ice-cold shower for five minutes before I could open my eyes. Managed to stay awake until 4.30 when I suddenly crashed. Unfortunately, I was right in the middle of an interview on the beach with a French TV crew. I almost literally fell face-forward into the sand when the journalist said, 'So many things I see in your interesting film. You have actor name Sam Rockwell and you have beautiful images like painter Norman Rockwell.'

Dead silence.

I stared at him in numb disbelief. He stared back, growing more and more nervous by my silence. I looked around at the Adriatic behind me, bright blue and rippled with small wind waves. Before me rose the fairytale hotel, its lacy terrace still packed with tight, shifting knots of people. Suddenly a stunningly voluptuous blonde ran by me, wearing a tiny navy blue bikini. Her golden hair rippled out behind her as her long tanned legs propelled her effortlessly across the hard packed sand. It was everything I could do to keep from ripping all my clothes off and running after her.

WEDNESDAY 11 DECEMBER

Despite the strong audience and critical response at Venice, no US distributor was re-inspired to buy the film. Turturro did not win Best Actor. A week later, *Box of Moonlight* screened at the Toronto Film Festival, to a sold-out house. Turturro joined me on stage afterwards and could not have been more supportive or complimentary.

Once again, no US distributor approached us. However, Geoff Gilmore, head of the Sundance Film Festival, saw the film in Toronto and invited it to Sundance as a special première. He was also surprised we didn't have a distributor.

'It's not as if one could look at your film and say, well if the story had been better, or if the acting or writing had been better – everything is strong. You made a good film. You've made a film about America that many people have tried to make but no one has succeeded. The only consolation I can offer is that the market for independent film right now is very bad. Independent distributors are looking for films that are sure bets, that will explode at the Box Office.'

THURSDAY 23 JANUARY 1997

Writing this on the plane back to NYC. Just took off from Salt Lake City. A storm last night dumped eight inches of snow on the area, making the mountains below me look like gigantic mounds of pure, white sugar.

In my lap is a copy of today's *New York Times*. Janet Maslin, the *Times* chief film critic, has written an article about this year's Sundance Film Festival, which I've now read about eight times.

Tom DiCillo has one of the festival's most hair-raising hard-luck stories, as well as one of its most likable films, the artfully whimsical *Box of Moonlight*, which was five years in the making and had been repeatedly passed on by the bigger independent distributors. (Trimark, a lower-profile distributor, bought it yesterday.) But Mr DiCillo came here prepared for the worst, even though his delightful *Living In Oblivion* was one of Sundance's biggest successes two years ago.

Box of Moonlight, with a quixotic magic, reminiscent of the Scottish film-maker Bill Forsyth's *Local Hero*, sends a straight-arrow electrical engineer (played by John Turturro) on a wild voyage of self-discovery. His companion is a long-haired renegade played by Sam Rockwell, who is so good in the film that he has been wandering around Sundance hearing the mating cry of the client-poaching Hollywood agent ('Are you happy?' 'Are you OK?').

'He's a movie star,' affirmed Harvey Weinstein of Miramax, who knows a thing or two about new talent. Mr DiCillo, also good at spotting star potential, found Mr Rockwell during auditions for his *Johnny Suede* but later gave the title role to the equally unknown Brad Pitt.

Mr Rockwell, who has shades of the same Pitt magnetism, faced the challenge of trying to keep his hair long for years as he waited for Mr DiCillo to raise enough money to make the film. Meanwhile, Mr DiCillo resisted the suggestion that he cast Jason Priestley and fumed about financiers and distributors who turned him down.

'Because this looks like it's happening,' he said of the sale to Trimark, 'I feel this extremely odd urge to punch some of these other people here. But I can't, because I've learned that if you're going to be in this business, you've got to be able to digest feathers, beaks and gnarly, wrinkled claws. You have to learn to eat crow.'

Box of Moonlight screened at Sundance on Monday night. Trimark made us an offer immediately after the screening. The deal was signed on Tuesday and on Wednesday morning an article appeared in *Variety* announcing the sale. The sense of relief has left me weightless, almost inebriated. The film will finally be seen.

I've already begun telling people about the important lesson I've learned: never present a film to distributors without the support of a major US festival. At a festival like Sundance, a hot film creates a buzz that forces distributors to take chances. They're so worried that another distributor will get the hot film that for once they act without thinking. I'm convinced now this is the only way to get a film like *Box of Moonlight* into the theaters.

However, I also know this is a lesson valid only in hindsight. I still wake up at night thinking about the tremendous joy I felt on first seeing the Opening Credit sequence with Jim Farmer's exquisite new music. I will never forget my original belief, before any distributors had passed on it, that I really had made a film people would want to see. I will never forget my original conviction, after first seeing audiences respond to the brilliantly human performances of John Turturro, Sam Rockwell and Catherine Keener, that I had made a film that could really touch people.

Box of Moonlight

CREDITS

AERIAL SHOT: *Camera passes over rural America; grasslands, wooded hills, an occasional small house. Late afternoon light gleams off the surface of lakes and streams as the camera sweeps low over the countryside. The sense of flying is emphasized.*

Main titles.

EXT. WOODS. AFTERNOON

DISSOLVE *to a tracking shot in a quiet forest. Deep yellow sunlight slants through gently shifting foliage.*

Light falls upon a Fawn nosing through fallen leaves. The camera moves toward it and passes so closely we see it is fake; a wide-eyed ceramic Bambi.

The camera emerges from the woods into a meadow. As credits end, camera cranes up over a small rise to reveal an industrial building under construction. Workers move about. Distant sounds of their voices, power tools, generators. A battered yellow school bus is parked off to the side.

INT. CONSTRUCTION SITE. PAINTROOM. LATER

Two uniformed workers lazily stack five-gallon cans of paint. On the backs of their jumpsuits a bright red thunderbolt with the words ZEUS POWER SYSTEMS. *Just then, Al Fountain strides purposefully through an open doorway. Al is Chief Electrical Engineer and is supervising construction on the entire job. His hard-hat displays his name and job title beneath a Zeus Power Systems logo (a bright red lightning bolt). He stands tall, erect; like the captain of a ship. He is about thirty-seven, strong, attractive, with a face of open, unshakable honesty.*

As he walks up, the workers mutter to themselves.

> FURMAN
> Look out, here he comes.

85

CHESTER
Probably gonna tell us how to stack the paint.

AL
Hold it, guys. Let me give you a hand there. There we go,
keep them nice and tight up against the wall with a one-inch
interval between the cans. That's the way.

*In showing the men how to stack the paint, Al actually stacks half the
cans himself. Al is about to continue through the room when he suddenly
hears an odd 'whack!' coming from behind a closed door.*

INT. CONSTRUCTION SITE. TURBINE ROOM. LATER

*Al marches into a large, cavernous room. At one end, a gigantic yellow
turbine is in the midst of installation. A huge clock hanging on a stand
shows the time to be 4.45 p.m. At the other end of the room Al sees a
group of Workers playing baseball; using a pipe for a bat and a wad of
duct tape for a ball. Their uniforms are also emblazoned with the Zeus
Power Systems thunderbolt.*

*Just then the tapeball goes flying through the air and rolls to a stop at
Al's feet. The Workers stop immediately and grin nervously at Al.
Soapy, an affable black man in his late forties, runs up. Soapy is Al's
foreman; he also wears a hard-hat with his name and job title printed
on it. He appears to have been pitching.*

SOAPY
Hey, Al!

AL
What's going on here, Soapy?

SOAPY
Not too much. Just messin' around. You know, a little game,
amusement . . .

AL
I suggest that you postpone this little game and get back to
work, pronto.

*Dex, one of the younger workers mutters under his breath, loud enough
for Al to hear.*

DEX

Christ, it's a quarter to fuckin' five!

AL

That's correct. Which means we have exactly fifteen more minutes to get that turbine squared away for a Systems Check. We're on a tight schedule here, guys. Now come on, work with me.

SOAPY

You got it, Al. We're with you. Alright fellas, break it up. That turbine's goin' in fifteen minutes.

INT. SCHOOL BUS. AFTERNOON. LATER

Most of the workers are laughing and talking loudly. Al sits by himself. He overhears Soapy speaking to some guys a few seats away.

SOAPY

Hey Dex. Poker game tonight. My room.

DEX

I'm there.

SOAPY

You come too, Taco; and bring Elwood with you. And some beer.

Al is not invited. His response to this exclusion is to turn suddenly to the window and stare intensely out at nothing.

EXT. SMALL HOTEL. EVENING. LATER

The yellow bus pulls up to a bland contemporary hotel on the outskirts of a small town. As Al exits the bus, Dex accidentally bumps into him.

DEX

What the fuck! Oh, sorry, man. I mean, Mr Fountain.

AL
(*forced laugh*)
It's alright, Dex, no harm done. You can call me Al, you know.

Dex runs ahead without answering and Al enters the hotel last, alone. Camera pans to a cheap Plexiglas marquee exclaiming: DRIP ROCK WELCOMES ZEUS POWER SYSTEMS JUNE 2–JULY ????

INT. HOTEL ROOM. NIGHT

Camera holds on a wide-angle of Al's hotel room. His voice can be heard humming, accompanied by the sound of a running shower. The camera pans past an open closet revealing six identical pairs of blue trousers next to six identical white shirts. Camera continues into the small bathroom, coming to rest on the closed curtain of a small pre-fab shower. From behind the curtain running water and Al's voice are heard.

> AL
>
> Sure, I'd love to play poker with you guys. I'll bring the beer! I insist; I'm the boss; I'll pay for the beer! Poker? No, I really have no desire to play poker with you guys. Why? Because it's a stupid game! You heard me; it's a stupid, stupid game!

Al violently rips the shower curtain back and steps out. He wraps a towel around him and vehemently begins combing his hair. We see his toiletries are neatly arranged on the sink.

Al stops suddenly and leans into the mirror. His fingers isolate a single gray hair which he plucks, and stands looking down at it in stunned amazement. CU: *the gray hair floating silently to the floor.*

INT. HOTEL DINING ROOM. NIGHT. LATER

Al sits alone in the hotel restaurant eating dinner. On one side of the room Soapy, Dex and the rest of the workers eat at a noisy, crowded table. Al's attention is suddenly drawn to a nearby table where a Waitress is filling a water glass. To his utter surprise he sees the water flow backwards up into her pitcher, leaving the glass empty. He is so disturbed by this he doesn't notice Soapy standing beside him.

> SOAPY
>
> What are you thinking about over here, Al?

> AL
>
> Oh, nothing really. Just thinking. What can I do for you, Soap?

I wanted to tell you I'm sorry about the incident today, Al.
Guys were just letting off a little steam. Won't happen
again.

AL
(*forced laugh*)
It's alright, Soapy; I understand. Sometimes I feel like doing
the same thing myself.

SOAPY
Well hell, why don't you come by the room and play some
poker tonight?

Al is so startled by the invitation he sits speechless.

AL
Poker? Maybe so. I've got a couple things to get squared away
but we'll see.

Soapy stares at Al for a moment then walks away.

INT. AL'S HOTEL ROOM. NIGHT. LATER

*Al re-enters his hotel room, noticing a pink card on the carpet as he
closes the door. Picking it up he reads* LOVE PHONE *printed beneath a
photo of a nude woman caressing a telephone. Al absently tears the card
into pieces and flushes them down the toilet.*

CU: *the brightly colored pieces of paper whirling around the toilet bowl.*

INT. AL'S HOTEL ROOM. NIGHT. LATER

Al sits alone on the hotel bed staring at his watch. Extreme CU *of the
watch: it is five seconds to 8 p.m. The moment the gigantic second hand
jerks up to the 12, Al picks up the phone and dials. Camera moves to a
small photo next to the phone showing Al standing next to his wife Deb,
with his arm around the tensed shoulder of his eight-year-old son,
Bobby. In the photo Bobby appears considerably less than happy.*

INT. THE FOUNTAIN HOME. NIGHT. LATER

Cut to a CU *of a color computer monitor. An elaborate martial arts video game is in progress, complete with sound effects. A phone is heard ringing over the sound of the game.*

CUT TO *a wider shot of a small boy sitting in front of the computer in the living room of a lower-middle-class home. He quickly puts the game on 'pause' and picks up the phone. Bobby is a slightly old-looking eight-year-old, with anxiety adding several years to his face. He is wearing a pair of pajamas three sizes too small for him.*

>   BOBBY
> Hello.

>   AL
> Hello, Bob, it's your father. What are you doing?

>   BOBBY
> Studying.

Deb appears in the doorway behind Bobby and stands watching her son. She is thirty, attractive and dressed in sweatpants and a T-shirt.

>   AL
> Good for you. See that? Summer school's not so bad, is it?

>   BOBBY
> No, sir.

>   AL
> What's twelve times seven?

>   BOBBY
> Seventeen.

>   AL
> I'm sorry, Bob. What'd you say?

>   BOBBY
> Twenty-eight.

>   AL
>   (*winces, almost in agony*)
> No it isn't Bob. Put your mother on.

Bobby hands the phone to his mother and goes immediately back to his video game, turning the sound down low.

DEB

Hi, Al.

AL

Is he studying, Deb? I don't get the sense that he's studying!

DEB

He's studying, Al.

Deb glances over at Bobby whose face is now only a few inches away from the computer screen.

AL

Well, I want you to get him some flashcards and I want him to know his multiplication, one through twelve, by the time I get home.

DEB

Did you have a bad day, Al? You seem a little tense.

AL

No, I had a good day, Deb. I had to get firm with some of the men but they took it well, which is good. I'm trying to instill in them a healthy respect for authority.

DEB

I'm sure they all like and respect you, Al.

AL

Well, that's not my concern.
(*chuckles*)
Although they did invite me to a poker game tonight.

DEB

Al, that's great. Are you going to go?

AL

No, I don't think so.

DEB

Oh, come on, Al. You should go.

AL

Listen, Deb. I'll go if I want to go. If I don't want to go then I'm not going to go.

                           DEB
No, you're right. Al. I'm sure you'll do whatever it is you
want to do.

                            AL
Yes. Well, we're right on schedule here and it looks like I'll be
home in six days.

                           DEB
For the fourth?

*Bobby turns away from the computer game and looks at his mother. She
shakes her head in a silent 'no' as Al replies.*

                            AL
No, we'll work that weekend and I'll fly out on the fifth.
Should get into Chicago about four thirty-eight.

                           DEB
I miss you, Al.

                            AL
Well, it's my job, Deb.

                           DEB
You're right. It's a good thing I didn't say something really
stupid like: I love you.

                            AL
And I love you too, Deb.

                           DEB
Hold on, Bobby wants to say something.

                          BOBBY
Dad, could I get some fireworks?

                            AL
No, Bob. Fireworks are illegal.

INT. AL'S HOTEL ROOM. NIGHT. LATER

Al places his ABCOM Specifications Manual *on the bed, then moves
to the window while unbuttoning his shirt. In a room a few floors below
him he sees an Old Man gazing out the window, unbuttoning his shirt.*

                            92

their movements are almost identical. The Old Man notices Al and
waves sadly with a lonely smile. Al's only response is to turn quickly
away from the window.

Al stands motionless in his room. He seems oddly disturbed. Suddenly he
rebuttons his shirt and exits his room.

INT. HOTEL HALLWAY. NIGHT. LATER

Al walks down the hotel corridor chuckling lightly and talking to
himself.

AL

Hey, guys. How's it going? How's it going, guys. Look out,
Fountain's here . . . hold on to your money.

Al pauses outside a partially open door. Sounds of men playing poker.
Al is about the enter when he hears Dex's voice.

DEX

What the hell did you invite Fountain for?

SOAPY

Don't worry, he's not going to show. He's probably in bed
right now with his nose stuck in the *ABCOM Manual.*

TACO

He's probably jerkin' off to it.

Huge burst of laughter.

ELWOOD

Hell, I bet he don't even jerk off.

DEX

He better not show up. The guy bugs the shit out of me.

SOAPY

Why?

DEX

He's an asshole!

SOAPY

I don't know, Dex. The way I see Al is he's just one of those

93

guys who goes through life like a robot. He can't help it; he's like a damn machine on auto-pilot. I feel kind of sorry for him.

                              DEX
Yeah? I still think he's an asshole.

                              TACO
So do I.

                              SOAPY
You may be right.

Al is so devastated he cannot move. Finally he backs away from the door and walks slowly down the hall to his room.

EXT. CONSTRUCTION SITE. MORNING

The camera follows Al as he stumbles around site. He looks exhausted completely disoriented. Soapy approaches him.

                              SOAPY
Turbine's in and all set for the Systems Check. So, whenever you want to give her the juice, just let me know.

                              AL
OK. Right. Systems check. We'll get that squared away right now.

                              SOAPY
Jesus, what'd you do Al; party all night?

                              AL
No, little trouble sleeping, that's all.

                              SOAPY
You should have come by the game.

                              AL
Yeah, I probably should have.

The two men stare at each other for a long moment. Al looks like he could strangle Soapy or break down in tears. Soapy senses something.

The sound of a helicopter suddenly interrupts them. All work stops as a helicopter lands amid a cloud of dust. The word ZEUS *is painted on its side, with a bright red thunderbolt passing through it.*

Al runs toward the helicopter. He speaks briefly to a well-dressed, white-haired woman seated beside the pilot, though nothing can be heard above the roar of the rotors. The woman hands Al a briefcase. Al steps back as the helicopter quickly takes off.

Moments later all is quiet again on the site. The Workers watch Al walk towards them with the briefcase. He appears even more confused and distracted.

SOAPY

What's goin' on, Chief?

AL

The job is canceled.

SOAPY

Canceled? What do you mean 'canceled'?

AL

Management decision. They're giving us all a bonus and sending us home.

Al hands Soapy the briefcase and walks off.

INT. SCHOOLBUS. DAY. LATER

The yellow school bus roars down the road. Inside, Soapy passes out personalized envelopes from the briefcase. Some workers have opened theirs and are counting large amounts of cash. Al sits by himself, staring absently out the window.

CUT TO: *Al's lap. He holds his envelope unopened.* CU: *Al's envelope. Typed on it:* 'ZEUS THANKS MR ALBERT FOUNTAIN.'

SOAPY

'Dexter Claggert'. There you go, Dex. Good job. Pass that back. Now listen up; the shuttle van leaves for the airport at three forty-five and you better be on it, cause I am not missin' that fuckin' flight.

95

TACO

Hey, Soap. We gonna come back later and finish this thing up?

SOAPY

Nope, they pulled the plug on it, Taco. Just gonna leave it sit. High level managerial decision. Right, Al?

Al nods once in response to Soapy, not looking at him.

I'd like to take a moment and thank our chief for gettin' us out of this shithole early with a bonus on top of it. Let's hear it for Al Fountain.

There is a very weak smattering of applause from the workers on the bus.

Now some of you might want to call your wives and girlfriends and let 'em know you're comin' home a week early; so you don't walk in on 'em unexpected. Elwood, I'm talkin' to you especially.

As Soapy continues, Al stares out the window of the moving bus. The bus passes a Small Boy, riding a beat-up old bike. Al is very surprised to see the boy and bike are moving backwards. He glances quickly around the bus to see if anyone else has noticed. No one has.

EXT. HOTEL PARKING LOT. EARLY EVENING. LATER

HIGH-ANGLE *on Soapy, Dex, Taco and other workers piling into several airport shuttle vans in front of the hotel. Suitcases being loaded in. Camera pulls back to reveal Al standing in his hotel room looking out the window. As the vans depart Al turns away from the window, a flicker of panic in his eyes.*

INT. THE FOUNTAIN HOME. NIGHT. LATER

Bobby leaps off the couch wearing only his underwear and a cape made from a bathtowel. Deb is stretched out on the floor reading a book and drinking a beer. When the phone rings, she leisurely reaches out to pick it up. Beside the phone is an enlarged photo of the family, identical to the one Al carries.

                              AL

Hi Deb, it's Al.

                              DEB

Mr Clockwork.

                              AL
                          (*startled*)

What?

                              DEB

It's eight on the button. I could almost set my watch by you.

                              AL

Didn't we say I could call at eight?

                              DEB

It's a joke, Al.

                              AL
                    (*a strained laugh*)

Oh, I see. Now I get it.
                        (*he doesn't*)

Listen Deb, I can't talk too long. I just wanted to let you
know we had a good day today and we're right on schedule.
Looks like I'll be seeing you in exactly six days.

                              DEB

Thanks for keeping me posted. What are you doing this
weekend?

                              AL

Oh, I don't know. I might go fishing with some of the guys.

                              DEB

That's great. See? I told you they liked you. Did you play
poker last night?

                              AL

Yes, and it was a lot of fun. So that's it really. I'll call you the
day after tomorrow.

                              DEB

Don't you want to speak to Bobby?

AL

No. I mean yes, but I'm practically out the door here. Did you get him the flashcards?

DEB

I did, Al.

AL

Good, very good. Well. Goodnight, Deb.

Deb hangs up and looks at Bobby for a moment who is standing nearby watching her.

DEB

Your father says goodnight.

Camera moves closer to Bobby's troubled face.

INT. CIRCLE RENT-A-CAR OFFICE. MORNING

Al studies a map at the counter while Doris, a humorless woman in her late fifties finishes the paperwork for his car. Doris is dressed in a hot pink uniform with matching cap and name tag.

CU: *Doris's hand holding the car keys fastened to a hot pink plastic medallion with the Circle Rent-a-Car logo.*

AL

Listen, Doris. I'm looking for a lake called Splashy Lake.

DORIS

Never heard of it.

AL

Really? I went there as a kid. It was more of an amusement type of lake, with paddle boats, picnic tables, a big slide –

Al suddenly stops for a moment, lost in thought.

DORIS

A slide?

AL

Yeah, this big slide that you had to swim out to.

(*smiling*)
You'd go down this thing and it would send you flying
twenty, thirty feet out into the middle of the lake. It was
incredible, really. It was . . .

DORIS
There's a swimming pool over in Neeterboro. They got a
slide.

AL
Oh. OK. Well, thank you, Doris. Maybe I will check it out.

EXT. CIRCLE RENT-A-CAR PARKING LOT. MORNING. LATER

*Al pulls out the Circle parking lot and stops before entering the main
road. A massive cluster of signs reads* NORTH AND SOUTH; *another*
EAST AND WEST. *Al looks from one to the other in indecision.*

*Suddenly he shifts uncomfortably in his seat. Reaching behind him he
finds a cassette tape prodding into his back, left behind by a previous
renter. It is a home-made tape marked with crude handwriting, 'Eddie's
Mix'. He slips it into the car's tape deck. 'Wayward Nile' by the
Chantays starts playing. Al listens for a moment then pulls out of the
parking lot, heading north.*

INT. AL'S CAR. MORNING. LATER

AL
Just a little drive, that's all; a drive down the road. 'Life is a
drive down the road.' Al Fountain, Saturday, June 30,
9.55 a.m.

MONTAGE. INT./EXT. SHOTS OF AL DRIVING

*Music continues. Al stays on a rural two-lane highway, passing
numerous run-down stores selling fireworks. Exterior shot from the side
of the road. Camera pans as Al drives by, revealing an old sign
partially obscured by bushes. Barely legible:* SPLATCHEE LAKE, 200
MILES.

EXT. MOTEL. TWILIGHT

Al pulls into a motel typical of those built along what used to be main highways in the late fifties. Al gets out of his car and enters the dilapidated office.

INT. MOTEL OFFICE. TWILIGHT. LATER

The Old Man behind the counter watches as Al takes several bills from his bonus envelope and pays for the room.

AL

Have you ever heard of a place called Splashy Lake?

OLD MAN

No. But there's a Splatchee Lake fifty miles east on 108.

AL

Paddle boats, picnic tables, a big slide . . .?

OLD MAN

Oh yeah, all kind of amusements.

AL

I can't believe it! I've been looking all over for this place. I don't know why, really. I spent a couple days there when I was a *kid* and I just remember having a great time.

OLD MAN

Me too. My brother and I drowned a cat there once.

AL

Is that right? Listen, how's the food across the street?

OLD MAN

Best I ever ate.

INT. SMALL HIGHWAY RESTAURANT. EVENING. LATER

Al eats alone in a nearly deserted restaurant across the highway from the motel. The Waitress, a once attractive woman in her late thirties refills the coffee cup of a Woman sitting nearby.

WAITRESS

That pie almost looks homemade, doesn't it?

100

Al stares hard at the coffee cup.

CU: *the cup; coffee running backwards up into the pot. The waitress notices Al's gaze and approaches him.*

More coffee?

> AL

No, thanks.

> WAITRESS

I'm off in a half-hour. Thank God. First thing I'm going to do is get all my clothes off and take a nice, long, hot shower.

> AL

That sounds good.

> WAITRESS

You staying over at the motel?

> AL

Actually, yes, I am.

> WAITRESS

How's the hot water over there?

> AL
>
> I don't know; I haven't tried it yet. Why?

> WAITRESS
>
> Just curious.

The Waitress holds Al's gaze until he finally realizes why and looks away in embarrassment. After a moment the waitress walks off.

INT. MOTEL ROOM. NIGHT

Al stands in his motel room, brushing his teeth in his underwear. He's talking to himself.

> AL
>
> 'Just curious?' If she's just curious why the hell doesn't she just call the motel and ask them how the hot water is?! What did she think? I was just going to invite her over here so she could take a shower?!

A sudden movement near the door draws his attention. Al looks over just as a pink card slips under the door and comes to rest on the stained carpet. When he picks it up he sees it is identical to the 'Love Phone' card he found in his hotel room.

Al opens his door and looks out. He sees nothing but a middle-aged couple asleep outside their door. The sound of a TV evangelist seeps from their room.

He shuts the door and stands in front of it, staring down at the pink card.

INT. MOTEL ROOM. NIGHT. LATER

CU: *the phone; the pink card now lies beside it. Camera pulls back to reveal Al sitting on the bed in his underwear. Cautiously Al dials.*

> VARLA
>
> (*voice-over*)
>
> Hello, I'm Varla and I'm lonely. Who are you?

> AL
>
> Norman.

VARLA
(*voice-over*)

What a sexy name. It's making me very hot and horny just
saying it, Norman. I can tell right now this is going to be a hot
and sexy call. Wait, there's someone at the door.
(*sound of a doorbell*)
Who could it be? I'm going to the door; I open it. Two men
rush in, their eyes red with lust. They rip my gown off,
exposing my naked body to their evil gaze. Just as they are
about to ravish me I stick my fingers into their eyes and rip
out both their eyeballs.

AL

Excuse me, Varla? Listen, I'm sorry but this isn't too
stimulating.

INT. PHONE SEX OFFICE. NIGHT

*A dark, tiny room. A young Woman sits at a desk in the shadows, fully
dressed, wearing a long, black Cher wig. A toy xylophone and several
sheets of paper lie on the desk. At Al's words a look of panic crosses her
face. She brings a mallet down on a xylophone key.*

CUT TO: *the top sheet of paper on Varla's desk. In a blank space at the top of the page we see she has penciled in the word 'Norman'. Camera moves slowly over the paper, revealing everything she has said so far (including the xylophone cue) and her following speech has been written down in meticulous handwriting.*

> VARLA

There's that doorbell again. I open the door, and oh, it's you, Norman. You stand there staring at me. I'm totally naked except for two bleeding human eyeballs in my hands. You say, 'Varla I've never seen a more beautiful, hot, sexy woman.' Say it Norman. Say it now.

INT. MOTEL ROOM. NIGHT. LATER

Al sits holding the phone in silence. Al abruptly and quietly hangs up. Extreme WIDE SHOT of Al in his underwear slouched alone on the bed.

INT. AL'S CAR. MORNING

The rural landscape rushes past. 'Too Much Tequila' by The Champs blasts from the tape deck. Al appears in an unusually good mood, tapping his fingers on the steering wheel and ad-libbing along with the music.

> AL

'It's not where you're going but how you get there that counts.' Al Fountain. Wait a second. 'It's not how you get there but where you're going that counts.' Is that right? Jesus Christ, what is it? 'Wherever you're going, I hope to Christ you get there!' Al Fountain, Sunday, July 1, 11.23 a.m.

Al's eyes focus suddenly on something in the distance. POV through the windshield: a large sign proclaiming SPLATCHEE LAKE. As it gets closer details of the old painted sign become clearer; kids in paddleboats, kids on a huge slide that shoots them out into the middle of a beautiful blue lake. Camera holds on the sign until it rushes by the car.

> AL
> (whispers)

Splashy Lake.

EXT. SPLATCHEE LAKE. DAY. LATER

Al's car moves slowly along a weed-strewn road of cracked asphalt.

The car pulls up to the edge of the lake and stops. Al gets out and stands motionless.

Splatchee Lake has been abandoned for years. The pebbly beach is strewn with litter. Several overturned and rotting paddleboats lie half-submerged in the oily water. A hundred yards away the huge rusting slide leans dangerously, creaking in the wind.

Al sits slowly at a broken picnic table with peeling white and yellow paint. In the distance a Couple strolling on the beach slowly move in Al's direction.

EXT. SPLATCHEE LAKE. PICNIC AREA. DAY. LATER

A moment later the Couple stop a few yards from Al. They're both middle-aged, both wearing identical skyblue vinyl windbreakers. The man has an official Boy Scout hatchet and holster attached to his belt.

> MAN
>
> Hello there! You're not contemplating a swim are you?

> AL
>
> No, I'm not.

> MAN
>
> Wife thought you were going in. There's a chemical plant around that cove that's been dumping formaldehyde in the lake for fifteen years.

> WOMAN
>
> You step in, it'll burn your feet right off.

> AL
>
> Jesus. Thanks for telling me.

> MAN
>
> No problem, just didn't want to have to go in after you. I'm Luvven Coddle, this is my wife, Wynelle.

> AL
>
> Hi, Al Fountain.

LUVVEN

Can I ask you; is everything alright, Al?

AL

Oh, sure; everything's fine. I haven't been here since I was a
Kid and it's kind of a shock to see it like this.

WYNELLE

I can imagine. We're used to it; we walk here every day.

*Luvven and Wynelle sit at the picnic table with Al. Luvven removes his
hatchet and begins absently chipping away part of the table.*

LUVVEN

I'm not used to it. It was a beautiful lake. Ever go down that
slide, Al?

AL

Yes, I did.

LUVVEN

Me too. Just like flying, wasn't it? Like a bird out over that
water.

Al looks at Luvven in amazement.

AL

That's exactly what it was like; flying. I remember shooting
down there and flying, my God, it must have been –

LUVVEN

Twenty . . . thirty feet.

AL

Yeah! Right out into the middle of the lake.

LUVVEN

Wasn't that water beautiful?

AL

It was incredible! Clean, clear. I remember my dad was
yelling for me to come in but I pretended like I didn't hear
him and just stayed out there. Finally he sent this *kid* out who
said, 'Your dad wants you to come in,' but I said, 'That's not
my dad,' and I kept going down that slide, even though I

knew he was going to give it to me as soon as I got in. It really did feel like flying.

LUVVEN

What do you mean, 'give it to you', Al?

AL

(*laughs*)

He pulled down my suit right here on the beach and spanked me with this slide rule he always carried around with him.

LUVVEN

I'm very sorry to hear that, Al. It must have been humiliating.

(*gently*)

Al, can I ask you: is there something else troubling you?

AL

What do you mean?

LUVVEN

Well, forgive me for prying, but I sense a yearning in you; a searching, almost as if you're lost, and you've been lost for a long, long time. Am I right?

Al is startled by the depth of Luvven's compassion. Looking at Wynelle he sees encouraging sympathy in her eyes too. He nods, on the verge of tears.

Have you found Jesus, Al?

In an instant Al sees the whole conversation has been a set-up. His face becomes rigid with anger.

AL

Why, is he missing?

WYNELLE

No. He's right here with us, Al.

AL

Oh, I thought I saw somebody walking on the water over there.

(*laughs*)

LUVVEN

I don't think your Salvation is a laughing matter, Al.

There is a creepy, malignant chill in Luvven's voice that brings Al to his feet. He looks like he wants to scream his outrage at Luvven but all that comes out is:

AL

Have a nice day!

Luvven and Wynelle sit motionless in the foreground as Al walks away from them and gets into his car. Wynelle's hand drops gently on to Luvven's and after a moment his grip on the hatchet relaxes.

INT. AL'S CAR. DAY. LATER

Al races down an empty two-lane road.

AL

Some people; man. They've got to stick their nose – why they can't just mind their own – but no, that's not enough. They have to – how about the salvation of your ass, pal, when I stick my foot up it!

Al's car continues accelerating. Suddenly he rounds a curve and sees an old convertible stalled right in the middle of the road. Al screams, slams on the brakes and jerks the wheel hard to the left. His car goes into a wild spin, turning 360 degrees before jerking to a stop.

EXT. ROADSIDE. DAY. LATER

A young man stares at Al in fascination, half hidden by the open front hood of his car. Kid is dressed completely in buckskin, with fringed jacket and pants, both worn and spotted with stains. He even has on a ratty coonskin cap. Except for the cheap dirty sneakers he looks like a young Davy Crockett. He beams at Al as he gets out of his car.

KID

Wow! That was great, man! Where'd you learn how to do that?!

                              AL
                         (*screaming*)
What the hell were you doing?!

                              KID
What do you mean?

                              AL
Stopping in the middle of the road like that! You almost got
us both killed!

                              KID
Oh, man. I'm sorry. My car just died on me and I can't move
her. I think blowed a gasket, or maybe it's that dang
carburetor. Know anything about engines?

                              AL
A little bit.

Al begrudgingly walks over to the Kid's car.

Out of the way.

*Al immediately snaps off the distributor cap and turns the distributor,
which spins freely.*

You've got trouble, pal.

                              KID
It's the gasket, right?

                              AL
No, it's your distributor. The drive gear is broken.

                              KID
Shit. What are we gonna do?

Al is a little surprised at the 'we'.

                              AL
I guess I'll have to drive you to a service station.

                              KID
What about the car?

                              AL
You'll have to leave it.

                              KID
No, I've got to get her home.

                              AL
Yeah, well, how do you propose to do that?

                              KID
I got a chain in my trunk.

Al stares at the Kid for a long moment.

EXT. ROADSIDE. DAY. LATER

CUT TO: *a thick, rusty chain being worked through the bumpers of both cars. Camera pans to reveal Al kneeling between the two cars, wrestling with the chain.*

Suddenly Kid appears silently just behind Al, watching him intently. He's holding something heavy in his hand.

MID-SHOT: *the back of Al's head. Kid steps closer and raises his hand holding the object. He swings huge, old padlock in front of Al.*

                              KID
Here you go, man. Slap this on her. And you better lock it; could pop off.

                              AL
                       (*closing the lock*)
I assume you've got a key?

                              KID
                          (*alarmed*)
Oh shit!

                              AL
Goddammit! Why'd you tell me to –

                              KID
                          (*laughs*)
Course I got a key, man. What do you fuckin' think? Now come on, we got to figure out who's going to drive.

                                AL

What do you mean?

                                KID

Well, someone's got to ride the brake back here. But I know
the road better than you do. It gets a little tricky once we hit
the woods.

                                AL

I thought you said you just lived up the road.

                                KID

Yeah, up the road and a couple few miles through the woods.

                                AL

Alright, you drive. But be careful; that's a rented car and I'm
responsible for it.

                                KID

Hey, I hear that. Name's Bucky, by the way. But some people
call me the Kid, or just Kid.

Al begrudgingly shakes the Kid's hand.

                                AL

Al Fountain.

                                KID

Hey. Alright, Al. I really appreciate this.

                                AL

Let's get going; I've got to be someplace.

*As the Kid gets into the rented car, Al gets into the convertible and
glances around the littered interior. A large ceramic stag with antlers
stands in the back seat, half covered with a blanket. Suddenly Al spies a
huge box of assorted fireworks beside a half-empty pint of Jack Daniels.*

                          (*disgusted*)

Jesus Christ.

*'Mexican Radio' by Wall of Voodoo suddenly comes blasting out of Al's
car. The Kid leans out the window grinning.*

                              KID
Hey, that's some weird shit, Al!

                               AL
Come on, let's go!

The car jerks forward almost snapping Al's neck.

    Easy!!

The Kid leans out again, laughing.

                              KID
    Sorry, Al. I got it now.

The two cars lurch forward, gradually picking up speed. Al appears very uncomfortable driving Kid's car, especially with the stag looking over he shoulder. Kid meanwhile drives with one hand, slapping the outside of the car in time to the music from Eddie's Mix.

MONTAGE. KID TOWS AL. DAY TO EVENING

Various exterior shots of the two cars moving down the road. Time passes. The sun sets. The shots accentuate the image of Al being towed, pulled forward.

EXT. KID'S TRAILER. NIGHT

It is after dark when Kid stops at the end of a wooded dirt road. The car headlights illuminate a dilapidated mobile home. Al and Kid get out of the cars.

                              KID
                           (*yawning*)
    Well, here we are, Al.

                               AL
You live here?

                              KID
Yup; own my own home. Ain't much, but I'm off the grid, man. That's what counts. Come on in. I'll turn on some lights.

AL

Look, just get the key and unlock these cars, OK? I've still got
to find a motel.

KID

Nearest one's a truckstop whorehouse off exit 58. Friend of
mine got syphilitis there just by turnin' on the TV. Hell, you
can stay here.

AL

No I can't. I've got a very important phone call to make.

KID

Shit, I got a phone. You can use it while I get the key.

INT. KID'S TRAILER. NIGHT. LATER

Al follows Kid in the front door and waits impatiently in the darkness.
A shadowy figure moves behind him silently. Suddenly a switch is
clicked and a series of lights come on. Al is astonished by what he sees.
Kid's house is actually only half a mobile home; the entire back is
completely open to the woods. Cheap furniture and junkyard belongings
spill outside into a clearing, faintly lit by colored bulbs strung between
trees.

AL

What the hell happened here?!

KID

What do you mean?

AL

Where's the rest of your house?

KID

I only bought half; got a really good deal. Now listen, when
you use the phone only talk for one minute. I'm tapped in
illegal and anything longer they can trace.
(*yawns*)
Christ, all that drivin' wore me out. I'm hittin' the sack. You
can have the bed.

113

Kid staggers out the back of the house and wrenches open an old fold-out couch beneath a tree.

> AL

Hey, wait a second.

> KID

No, I insist. You drove me all the way home; it's the least I can do.

Kid collapses on the couch and immediately falls asleep with his coonskin cap still on.

> AL

Hey. Hey, Buck. Give me the key. Kid. Buck. Kid. Hey, the Kid, where's the key?

There is absolutely no response. After a moment Al finds the phone and dials. He carefully eyes the second hand of his watch as he talks.

> AL
> (*whispers*)

Hello Deb. It's Al.

> DEB

Al! I'm so glad you called. Where are you?

> AL

Remember I told you I was going fishing? We're all in a little cabin together.

> DEB

That sounds great. Having a good time?

> AL

Great time. Listen, some good news: we're ahead of schedule and it looks like I'll be coming home early.

> DEB

Al, that's great! When?

> AL

Well, we're driving back to Drip Rock tomorrow; I'll probably spend the night and fly out on the 3rd.

                              KID

So we can have a 4th of July!

Al nervously checks his watch.

                              AL

It looks that way. I can't wait to see you, Deb. And now I
should go.

INT. THE FOUNTAIN HOME. NIGHT. LATER

                             DEB

Here, say 'hi' to Bobby.

                            BOBBY

Hi, Dad.

                              AL
                          (*quickly*)

Hi, Bob. What's up?

                            BOBBY

Dad, are the little fireworks illegal? You know, the real little
ones?

                              AL

They sure are, Bob. All fireworks are illegal.

                            BOBBY

I was just checking. Goodnight, Dad.

                              AL

Goodnight.

*As Al hangs up, Kid mumbles faintly from outside. Al casts the Kid a
wary glance then gets into bed fully dressed. The camera pulls back into
a* WIDE SHOT *that frames the mobile home with Al inside and Kid
asleep outside on the fold-out couch. Al turns out the light and the screen
goes black. Silence.*

INT. KID'S TRAILER. MORNING

A tremendous explosion. CUT TO: *Al jerking upright in bed. A
splintered metal bucket sails out of the sky and clatters to the ground.*

It takes a moment for Al to orient himself. He's in half a mobile home open to a clearing bright with morning sunlight. A moment later Kid walks around the corner of the trailer smoking a cigarette.

KID

Mornin'.

AL

What the hell was that?!

KID

M-80. Them suckers sure pack a whallop. Got the cars unlocked. C'mon man, get some breakfast before you take off.

The Kid opens the toy-like refrigerator and takes out a jumbo bag of Oreos and a carton of milk. He grabs some bowls and carries everything outside to a rickety table. Al staggers out to join him.

While Kid fills the bowls with cookies and milk, Al looks around. In daylight, Kid's house looks even more absurd, like it was struck by a tornado which ripped it in two and spewed things all around the clearing.

He sees they are eating on a child's pool table surrounded by mismatched barstools and one or two warped cues.

Beneath a tree a broken Lazy Boy recliner faces a TV with a cracked screen.

Numerous brightly painted ceramic statues of animals and cartoon characters adorn the clearing. The antlered stag is now out of Kid's car and standing alertly a few feet away from the table.

AL

How long have you lived here?

KID

I been off the grid now about three years. Dig in, before it gets too mushy. I know what you're sayin' though. Place could use a little work. See, I'm kind of in a intermediary stage. I want to go total self-sufficient; solar power, windmill, generate my own electricity. You know anything about that stuff?

                    AL

I know something about it.

                    KID

See that? I could tell you had a knack for things mechanical.
What do you do?

                    AL

I'm an electrical engineer, specializing in field installation of
Zeus Turbine Generators.

                    KID

No shit. I bet you'd even know how to change a distributor
drive gear. Am I right?

*Al stares at Kid for a moment who looks back at him with a hopeful
milk-wet smile.*

                    AL

Listen, Buck or Kid or whatever your name is, I went out of
my way to get you home last night and now I'm badly behind
schedule. I'll drop you off at the nearest garage. After that
you're on your own.

                                KID
    That's fine by me, Al. Really.

*The two men continue eating their breakfast in silence. Small birds hop
in and out of patches of sunshine around the outdoor table.*

INT. AL'S CAR. DAY. LATER

*Al drives while Kid stares moodily out the window. Eddie's Mix is in
the tape deck, playing Nick Cave's 'Red Right Hand'. Al keeps
glancing over at Kid.*

                                AL
    What's with the costume, Buck?

                                KID
                           (*surprised*)
    How'd you know it was a costume?

                                AL
    Is it?

                                KID
    Yeah, I was an actor for a while, in this play about Davy
    Crockett in the olden days.

                                AL
    You played Davy Crockett?

                                KID
    No, some guy standin' around with a rifle. But one night I
    tried on Davy's costume and it fit me so perfect I just took it.

                                AL
                           (*startled*)
    You stole it?

                                KID
    Pull up a second, Al.

EXT. ROADSIDE. NEAR A SMALL HOUSE. DAY

*Al stops in front of a small house set back from the rural road. Kid gets
out, lopes casually across the lawn and picks up a large ceramic dwarf.*

He returns to the car and puts the dwarf in the backseat.

                              AL
What's going on?

                              KID
Little business. I'm in salvage; specializing in field installation
of lawn ornaments.

*Just then an old man and woman come out of the house and stand
staring at the car, smiling in polite confusion.*

                              KID
Hey, there! Like that dress. Looks real fine on you.

                              AL
You know those folks?

                              KID
Oh yeah. I'm comin' back for them squirrels later. Alright,
you all take care now! Any time you want to move on is fine
by me, Al.

EXT. SMALL TOWN. DAY. LATER

*Moving shots out of the car side window. Closed gas stations, used car
lots, carpet warehouses with* GOING OUT OF BUSINESS *signs.*

EXT. LYLE'S GARAGE. DAY. LATER

*Al pulls into Lyle's Auto Repair, a small, run-down garage beside a
vacant lot littered with old tires. Al and Kid get out and approach Lyle
who is leaning into the open hood of a car. Kid greets him warmly.*

INT. LYLE'S GARAGE. DAY. LATER

                              KID
Hey, Lyle!

*Lyle stands up and looks at Kid with complete indifference. He's pale,
unshaven, with thinning oily hair.*

                             LYLE
What the fuck do you want?

119

                              KID
Blew my distributor, man. This is my friend, Al. He'll tell you
exactly what kind.

                               AL
I need a distributor drive gear for a '68 Pontiac LeMans.

Lyle looks at Al, then walks into the back of the garage.

*A rusting beat-up Chevy pulls up, its muffler dragging harshly on the
pavement. Two sullen men get out. Wick wears a leather vest over his
bare chest; his entire right arm is puckered and stretched with scar tissue
from a severe burn. Doob is tall and skinny with a filthy Bandaid
across the bridge of his nose.*

*Kid greets them warmly also, especially Wick. Al senses an obvious
tension between the two.*

                              KID
Hey Wick. Hey Doob. What's shakin?

                             WICK
My left nut.

Kid laughs with forced enthusiasm.

                              KID

Mine too. Hey, what're you guys doin' for the fourth?
Anything goin' on, any parties?

*Wick and Doob ignore Kid completely, moving over to a fan belt
display. Kid lights a cigarette and absently flicks the match to the floor
as Lyle returns with the drive gear.*

                             LYLE
$11.99.

CUT TO: *the match as it bounces a short distance and lands next to
Wick's foot. It flares briefly then goes out with a rising plume of smoke.
Wick suddenly whirls around.*

                             WICK
You throw that match at me?

KID

No, Wick.

DOOB

Yeah, he did.

KID

No, I just threw it down. You know, throwin' down a match,
that's all.

WICK

Don't you ever fuckin' do it again.

KID

I won't, Wick.

Al watches the two with mildly annoyed curiosity.

WICK

Where'd you get that fuckin' hat?

KID

(*laughs*)

All right, I'm out of here. Thanks a lot, Lyle. Wick, Doob –
you guys take it easy now.

EXT. KID'S TRAILER. DAY. LATER

Camera is close on the grinning face of the ceramic dwarf. Camera pulls back to reveal the dwarf is now standing in Kid's yard. Al bends into the hood of Kid's car while Kid waits eagerly beside him.

KID
I really appreciate this, Al.

Though Al is greasy and sweaty and does all the work, he doesn't seem to mind. His movements are quick and expert, as if he's enjoying showing off his knowledge of engines. He orders Kid around like a child.

AL
Alright, now give me the wrench.

KID
I'm gonna take a course or something on auto repair.

AL
A driver should know his car, Buck. See these two bolts?
They go on last. OK, start her up. Pump the gas once.

Kid quickly gets in the car and does as Al says. His car starts immediately.

KID
Look at that! You're a goddam wizard, Al.

AL
Turn it off now.

Suddenly a pick-up truck pulls into the yard and a short, fat man in his late fifties gets out.

KID
Got a customer, Al. Be right back.

Al picks up the tools, watching Kid and the man out of the corner of his eye.

Hey there, Navajo!

NAVAJO
Hey, Kid. What'ya got for me.

KID

I got this beauty right here.

The man moves over to the ceramic stag and inspects it like a dog show judge.

NAVAJO

Nice legs. Nice chest. Hell of a set of nice antlers. I think I'll take it.

He hands Kid some cash then puts the stag in his truck and drives off. Kid walks up and sees Al frowning at him.

KID

What's the matter?

AL

No receipt?

KID

What for?

AL

So you can calculate your income when you pay your taxes.

Kid suddenly cracks up.

KID

Taxes! Are you fuckin' crazy!? I never paid taxes in my life, and I never will, man! I tore up my goddam Social Security card. I got none of that shit now; no credit cards, no phone cards – hell, I don't even have a driver's license.

AL

Wait a second. You're driving without a license?

KID

I told you, man. I'm off the fuckin' grid!

AL

You're off your fucking nut! You get in an accident and you injure somebody, you're going to jail! Especially if you're driving intoxicated with a carload of illegal fireworks!

Al points to the interior of Kid's car, where the bottle of Jack Daniels

*still sits beside the now-opened box of fireworks. Kid stands quietly for a
moment, apparently genuinely distressed by Al's tirade.*

> KID
>
> You're right, Al. I don't know what I was thinkin'. I feel really
> stupid.

> AL
>
> Well, Buck, it's your life and frankly, it's none of my business.
> Now listen, is there someplace I can get washed up?

> KID
>
> Yeah, there's a big pool back in the woods. That's where I
> take a bath, plus it's good swimmin'.

> AL
>
> I'm not talking about swimming. I want to wash up and I
> want to get back on the road.

> KID
>
> That's what I'm sayin' Al. You jump in, get cleaned up and
> take off.

EXT. ROCK POOL. DAY. LATER

*Al and Kid emerge from the woods into a small clearing. Below them
lies a large pool carved out of the surrounding rocks by a quickly flowing
stream. Kid removes all his clothing with complete nonchalance.*

> KID
>
> There she is, Al. Water leans a bit to the cool side, but the
> Indians say it's good for your skintone.

> AL
>
> What Indians?

> KID
>
> Crowsfeet; they lived in this valley for centuries.

> AL
>
> The Crowsfeet?

> KID
>
> They were the first Indians to tame the wild dog.

124

AL

Is that a fact?

KID

Yup, I been studyin' all about that stuff. This is the best way in, Al. Right here.

Kid suddenly leaps off the rocks and plunges into the water below. He surfaces, blowing hard and dogpaddling.

Come on, Al. I'm out of the way.

Al hesitates for a moment then strips down to his underwear, looking cautiously around him as he does so. He moves to the edge of the rock and leaps off.

Underwater shot: slow-motion. Al plunges into frame. He comes up with a little smile on his face.

KID

Feel that skintone?

AL

Sure do.

Al is a good swimmer. He circles the pool a few times while Kid continues his dogpaddling.

This is a nice little spot, Buck.

KID

Not many people know about it; I guess. Most of the time I have it to myself.

HIGH-ANGLE SHOT *looking down on the pool. Al and Kid continue swimming lazily.*

EXT. TOMATO FIELD. DAY. LATER

It is about an hour from sunset when Al and Kid come out of the woods and enter a vast hilly field of tomatoes planted in long staked rows. A small farmhouse stands in the distance.

AL

I thought you said this was a short cut.

KID

Well, I never really timed it, Al. It just always seemed shorter.

Kid plucks a ripe tomato and takes a bite out of it.

Nothing like a tomato right off the vine. Try one, Al.

AL

Whose are they?

KID

Some old guy. He don't give a shit. I'm gonna take a leak.

Kid ambles off behind the plants as Al plucks a tomato and stands eating it, looking frequently toward the farmhouse. After a moment the simple, quiet tranquillity of the scene affects him and he smiles for the first time.

AL

'Life is a tomato right off the vine.' Al Fountain. Monday, July 2, 4.32 p.m.

KID

Hey, Al.

Just as Al turns around Kid throws a huge tomato at him. It hits him square in the chest, splattering red dripping goo all over his white shirt. He stares at Kid in stunned disbelief.

Sorry, Al. I thought you would duck.

Seeing the grin pulling hard on the corners of Kid's mouth, Al snaps. He is furious.

AL

You little fucking bastard!

Al whips his tomato at Kid as hard as he can. Kid barely manages to dodge it he's laughing so hard. He falls through a row of vines and scrambles to his feet as Al crashes after him, furiously grabbing tomatoes.

MONTAGE. TOMATO FIGHT. DAY. LATER

An intense tomato war ensues. The camera races through the rows with

127

128

Al and Kid as they hurl tomatoes at each other with the seriousness of soldiers in combat. Shots of tomatoes flying, tomatoes hitting bodies, Al and Kid crashing through the vines.

Al spies Kid lying in wait for him down in a little gully and he begins creeping stealthily toward him. He takes Kid completely by surprise and hits him right in the face with a big ripe tomato.

Just then they hear the crackle of a police bull-horn above them.

SHERIFF
Alright now, boys. Come on up outta there.

Kid grabs Al and pulls him down beside him. Peering up through the leaves they see an obese town Sheriff, a Patrolman and an old Farmer standing beside a squad car at the top of the gully.

AL
Jesus Christ. It's the police.

KID
Quiet!

AL
I thought you said nobody cared about these tomatoes?!!

SHERIFF
Let's go, boys. I can see one of your white shirts plain as day, so why don't you just stand up and let's get this over with.

Al starts to stand up. Kid jerks him back down.

KID
What the hell are you doin?! Take that shirt off!

Al is somewhat surprised by the intensity of Kid's command. He takes off his shirt and watches as Kid quickly drapes it over some plants. Then, motioning Al to stay very low, Kid crawls on his stomach down a row of tomatoes.

Kid leads Al around the bottom of the gully, circling up through the rows behind the police car. They peer out at the backs of the threesome standing beside the car. Its bubble lights are flashing, its doors are open and occasional squawks are heard from the radio.

SHERIFF

Alright, boys, I'm tired of this shit.
> (*to the Patrolman*)

Let's get 'em, Floyd.

Al and Kid watch the Sheriff and Patrolman leave the car and work their way down the side of the gully. The Farmer follows them cautiously.

AL

Come on, let's get the hell out of here!

KID

Hold on.

Kid slips out of the bushes and creeps up to the patrol car. Reaching into the open driver's side door, he releases the parking brake then dashes back into the bushes beside Al.

They watch as the squad car quietly begins to roll down the gully straight at the Farmer and two Lawmen. At the last moment they hear it and leap wildly out of the way.

Picking up speed the car passes them and crashes into the tomato field, heading straight for Al's white shirt.

SHERIFF

Goddammit, Floyd, you stupid son of a bitch! Get the car!
Look out boys! Get up! Run!

The sheriff watches in horror as the car plows through the shirt, continuing down the gully and finally coming to a stop at the very bottom of the field.

Oh Jesus, Jesus, God; we killed 'em!

EXT. KID'S TRAILER. EVENING. LATER

Al rushes out of Kid's open-air home carrying his suitcase and wearing a new shirt. Kid walks quickly behind him.

KID

I'm sorry, Al. Really, I was just trying to create us a diversion so we could get away. It's an old Indian trick.

AL

Yeah? Well, let me tell you, Buck; that little stunt of yours almost killed three people, two of whom were policemen. Not to mention the damage you undoubtedly did to their car!

Al throws his suitcase in the back seat and gets in his rented car. Kid stands dejectedly by the window.

KID

I never thought of it that way. You're absolutely right; it was pretty stupid. You must think I'm a worthless, fuckin' piece of shit.

AL

Look Buck, I like you but I've got to tell you something. I think it's time you got your life squared away.

KID

I think you're right, Al.

AL

Well, goodbye. And good luck.

KID

Goodbye, Al.

Al reaches out to start the car and finds the keys are not in the ignition. He looks on the seat, on the floor then jumps out of the car and checks all his pants pockets.

                              AL
Where the hell are the keys?!

                              KID
What, the car keys?

                              AL
Yes, the car keys!

                              KID
Alright, hold on, Al. When did you last have them?

                              AL
When I drove you into town.

                              KID
OK. We got back. You got out of the car. What'd you do with the keys?

                              AL
I thought I left them in the car.

                              KID
Might you have put 'em in your pocket?

                              AL
I might have.

                              KID
Damn. I bet they fell out when you were runnin' around in that tomato field.

                              AL
Oh, Christ!

                              KID
Al, take it easy. First light, crack of dawn, we go back to that field and find those goddam keys.

                              AL
I've got to get going!

KID

I know you do Al, and I'm damn sorry. I feel responsible.

INT. KID'S TRAILER. NIGHT. LATER

Night has fallen. Al is on the phone to his wife. Kid sits outside in the dark watching TV and poking a small fire. Again Al carefully watches his watch as he talks.

DEB

You're still there?!

AL

Hey, don't think I'm happy about this. I wanted to get the hell out of here yesterday.

DEB

I just bought sixty dollars' worth of groceries for a cook-out.

AL

Well, you and Bob get started and I'll try to be there. Don't let him start the fire. Now, how's he doing with the flashcards?

INT. THE FOUNTAIN HOME. NIGHT. LATER

Deb stands in the living room. Beyond her, Bobby paces, nervously studying a set of huge flashcards that he struggles to hold in two hands.

DEB

I'll let him tell you.

Deb hands the phone to Bobby, who shifts the flashcards under his arm. They are almost as big as he is.

BOBBY

Hi, Dad. Thanks for the flashcards. They're really helping a lot.

AL

Good. I told you they would. What's twelve times eight?

Bobby starts clumsily looking through the flashcards. He can't find twelve times eight. Al looks nervously at his watch.

133

Bob? You've got about ten seconds.

BOBBY

Fifteen.

AL

(*winces*)

Listen, Bob, I'm going to let you go now because it sounds like you've still got a lot of work to do.

EXT. KID'S TRAILER. CAMPFIRE. NIGHT

Al hangs up and walks out of the mobile home to join Kid by the TV. A couple of incinerated hotdogs lie smoking on the makeshift grill.

KID

Dig in, man. And save room for dessert.

Kid holds up a bag of marshmallows, not taking his attention off the wrestling match underway on the TV. Al spears a hotdog with a stick as Uncle Samson, dressed in red, white and blue trunks with shoulder-length blond hair, battles The InFidel, a Hispanic dressed in combat fatigues who looks just like Castro.

KID

You like wrestlin', Al?

AL

I like college or high school wrestling; not this garbage.

KID

Hey, this ain't no high school shit. It's professional wrestling.
That's my guy right there, Uncle Samson. He's ranked
number one by the WWF and the NWF both. Look at the
muscles on that sucker. He is tough and mean. Watch this.
Sam's gonna tear The InFidel apart.

*Kid loses himself completely in the match, ecstatic when Uncle Samson
is winning and agonized when he's not. When the ref isn't looking the
InFidel 'smashes' Sam over the head with a chair, then advances on
him with a huge pair of scissors intent on cutting his hair.*

Get away from there, you greasy bastard! You see what he
did, Al? Fightin' dirty; that's the only way he can win. You
blind egg-suckin' ref!

*Uncle Samson recovers in the nick of time and moments later he pins the
InFidel. Kid jumps out of his chair, chanting with the TV crowd.*

KID

Sam! Sam! Uncle Sam! What'd I tell you; Al? Tough, isn't
he? Shakin' off a blow to the head like that?

AL

You know it's all fake, don't you?

KID

What is?

AL

The whole thing; the kicks, the punches, the chair-smashing.
They plan out every fight; who's going to win and who's
going to lose. It's all fake. Everybody knows that.

Kid gives Al a sympathetic smile as if he's talking to a raving lunatic.

KID

Al, I know you're smart cause you got a scientific-style job,

135

but you're not using common sense. If this fight is fake, and
everybody knows it's fake, then why in the hell would
anybody waste their time sittin' around watchin' it?!
(*laughs*)

AL

That's a question you might want to answer one day, Buck.

*Kid turns the TV off, throwing the yard into much softer moonlight. He
goes to his car and comes back with the bottle of Jack Daniels.*

KID

I know the answer. And this is what's happenin' all over
America, Al. This country's bein' taken over by smart people
with no common sense. And that's why I'm out here, man.
Just me, my instincts and Nature. That's all you need. See
that moon up there? Shit, you're in the city, you wouldn't
even be able to see it.

AL

It's a three-quarter moon, just about to slip into its second
phase.

KID

Well, I don't know about that, but the Indians call it a
Creamy Corn Moon.

*The two stare up at the night sky for a long moment in silence. Suddenly
Al picks up the bottle of Jack Daniels and takes a pull on it.*

What are you thinkin' about, Al?

AL

It's kind of hard to say this, but I've started seeing things.

KID

What kind of things are you seein'?

AL

Well, I'm seeing things moving backwards. Like someone
pouring a cup of coffee; I'll see the coffee flowing out of the
cup back into the pot.

You're kiddin' me!?

No, other things too. I saw a kid riding a bike, pedalling just like normal, except he was moving backwards.

Jesus! That's wild, man!

I'm a little worried actually. I never know when it's going to happen.

Well, don't worry about it, Al. That's the main thing. The Indians saw shit all the time; they never worried about it. OK?

OK.

And don't worry about them car keys either. I know exactly where to look; right where we left your shirt.

Kid suddenly looks at an object on the ground a few yards away. He walks over and kneels beside a small lacquer box, old and beat-up yet with areas of fine detail still engraved in the wood. A narrow shaft of moonlight filters through the leaves and falls directly into the open box.

Hey, look what that moon's doin' over there. Watch this.

He closes the box.

Now I got a little box of moonlight. See how I did that, Al?

EXT. ROCK POOL. DAY

Al flies through the air in his underwear and splashes into the pool.

A moment later he climbs out of the pool and approaches Kid, dripping wet by the rocks.

KID

How's that hangover, man? Gone, right?

AL

Well, it's starting to go.

KID

I told you; it's this water. Damn, it's funny about those keys, Al. I thought sure we'd find 'em.

AL

I've got another plan, Kid. I'll call the rental office when we get back to the house. They'll call a local locksmith, give him the key code for the model number of my car and I'll have a new set of keys delivered in less than an hour.

KID

Damn, Al. That's a great idea. Why the hell didn't I think of that?

AL

It's called Planning Ahead, Kid. You should try it sometime.

Kid suddenly turns away and picks up a pair of women's underwear.

KID

Look at this; someone was here yesterday.

Kid inspects the underwear intently, then sniffs them lightly. He pauses, thinking hard for a moment.

KID

Size five; hundred percent cotton. She's fifteen, blond; either a cheerleader or a swimsuit model.

AL

Get the hell out of here.

KID

Smell.

AL

I'm not going to smell somebody's underwear.

KID

Come on; a little sniff. I'll show you something.

Kid hands the underwear to Al, who sniffs them cautiously.

(*quietly*)

Smell that?

AL

What?

KID

That kind of dry mustard smell mixed with bubblegum.

Al sniffs the underwear again.

AL

I don't smell anything.

KID

Jesus, Al. Your senses are gone, man. To my nose it's almost over-powering. See that? It's called Sensuary Atunement. You should try it sometime.

AL

OK, I'll start sniffing underwear every chance I get. Let's head on back, Kid. I want to make that call.

Kid puts the underwear back where he found them.

> KID

One more swing on the rope and we're out of here.

INT. KID'S TRAILER. DAY. LATER

CU: *Al's hand repeatedly underlining the license number on his Circle Rent-a-Car form.*

Camera pulls back to reveal Al on the phone inside Kid's house. Kid, back in his buckskin outfit and holding a rifle, assumes hunting poses in front of a broken mirror leaning against a tree.

Al finally hangs up and looks around him in annoyance.

> AL

'It's not where you're going in Life, it's how you get the hell out of there!'

> KID

What's that, Al?

> AL

Where the hell are these people at twelve in the afternoon!?

> KID

Lunch. Try 'em in an hour.

> AL

Is that gun loaded?

> KID

You bet your ass it is. You think I'm gonna let them FBI sneak up on me? No fuckin' way.

> AL

Well, just be careful with it.

> KID

Hey, I know how to handle a gun. Do you?

> AL

I've shot a gun before.

                    KID

Good. Let's go get me a rabbit or something.

                    AL

No, Kid. I want to make this call.

                    KID

Come on, you got an hour. Here, take this. I'll get a shotgun.
Plus, I want to show you something too, man. I'm gonna
open your eyes up.

EXT. WOODS. DAY. LATER

*Al and Kid stroll through the woods, cradling their rifles. With his
coonskin cap on Kid looks again like a juvenile delinquent Davy
Crockett. Al stops suddenly, seeing a small fawn quietly nibbling leaves
in the dappled sunlight.*

                    AL
                 (*whispers*)

Kid! Look at that.

                    KID

Wow. It's a little baby deer. Let's take a look.

*Kid and Al move quietly towards the fawn, which seems completely
unaware of their presence. As they get closer we see we are in the same
clearing as the opening shot of the film and in fact this fawn is the same
ceramic Bambi.*

                    AL
                 (*puzzled*)

It's fake. It's a statue.

                    KID
                 (*laughs*)
Looked real though, didn't it?

                    AL

Who put it here?

                    KID

Me, man; who do you think?

                              AL

It looks great there, Kid. Thanks.

                              KID

For what?

                              AL

For showing it to me.

                              KID

That's not what I wanted to show you. I got something that's
gonna blow your mind. You wanted proof? Well, here it is.

EXT. MEADOW. CONSTRUCTION SITE. DAY. LATER

*In a shot identical to the one from the beginning of the film Kid and Al
emerge from the woods into a wide meadow. Below them lies Al's old
construction site, now quiet and deserted. Al is dumbfounded.*

                              AL

What the hell!

                              KID

A CIA nerve gas factory; that's what the hell! They're makin'
nerve gas to use against their own people. OK? Does that
blow your mind?

                              AL

I don't believe it! I just spent two days driving in a goddam
circle!

                              KID

What are you talkin' about?

                              AL

This is the job I told you I was working on. Christ, the car
rental place is right in town.

                              KID

Wait a second. You worked here?

                              AL

For a month. It's not a nerve gas factory; it's a semi-
automated facility for the manufacture of windshield wipers.

                              143

KID

I don't believe that for a second.

AL

Alright, you want some 'proof'? Come on, I'll give you some 'proof'!

Camera stays wide as Al marches Kid down the meadow toward the plant in the distance.

INT. CONSTRUCTION SITE. TURBINE ROOM. DAY. LATER

Al and Kid enter the large room where Al had discovered Soapy playing baseball with the rest of his crew. Al leads Kid up to the half-installed turbine.

AL

This is a Zeus 8000 turbine generator, Kid. It doesn't make nerve gas; it makes electricity. And that electricity was going to provide the power for the entire assembly line.

KID

Makin' windshield wipers?

AL

That's right. And I suppose if you equipped enough people with windshield wipers they could probably take over the country.

KID

I can't believe you worked here, man. I could never do this shit. Didn't you hate it, always havin' some asshole boss tellin' you what to do?

Kid kicks the wad of duct tape Soapy was using for a ball, sending it rolling across the cement floor toward Al.

CU: *Al, watching the ball of tape rolling toward him, his face clouding suddenly in memory.*

CU: *the tape ball coming to a stop at Al's feet. Suddenly Kid calls out from across the room.*

Hey, Al, think you could hit that bottle over there.

AL

It's in front of the window.

KID

You can't hit it.

Al raises his rifle and shoots at a soda bottle standing on a window sill about thirty yards away. He misses the bottle and puts a small hole in the window.

Missed, Al. Let me try.

Kid lets go a blast from his shotgun and blows out the entire window.

AL

Jesus Christ, Kid, that's an $800 window!

Kid immediately turns and blows out another window.

KID

That's $1600 right there. What's in those cans?

AL

Paint.

145

KID

You sure?

Al suddenly fires a shot at the stacked rows of five-gallon cans. A fountain of white paint comes spurting out.

That's paint alright.

Kid steps closer to the cans and pumps three shells into them. The cans explode in a huge blast of metal and paint. Al also empties his rifle at the cans.

INT. SHOOTING MONTAGE. DAY. LATER

Al and Kid race around inside the building shooting everything that will break or explode.

Bullets smash into bottles, cans, windows, walls, barrels, hard-hats, glass pressure dials . . .

Various liquids spew out of blasted containers and run along the floor.

Windows explode, filmed from both inside and outside the building.

CU: *bullets being loaded, shells flying into the air, fingers on triggers, smoke curling from gun barrels.*

EXT. MEADOW. DAY. LATER

On a particularly violent explosion cut to blue. Camera pans down from the blue sky to reveal Al and Kid sprawled in the meadow with the plant visible below, wisps of gunsmoke drifting from its broken windows. Their guns lie in the grass beside them.

KID

You ever have a dog, Al?

AL

When I was a boy.

KID

I'm thinking I might get one. They're fun to have around, right? Always wagging their tails and making you play with them. What was your dog's name?

Barky. He was just a mutt, all white except for one black ear.
He found this rubber monkey somewhere and every day when
I came home from school he'd be sitting in the front yard
with that damn monkey in his mouth, waiting for me to throw
it for him. Kid, I'm telling you; I threw that monkey for
hours. He never got tired of chasing it.

KID

Still got him?

AL

Oh no, he died. I let him out one night, right before I went to
bed and when he came in he was shaking and breathing
funny. I asked my dad if we should take him to the vet but he
said no, it's after nine, the vet's probably closed. We'll take
him in the morning. So we went to sleep, and as soon as it
was light I looked under my bed, that's where Barky always
slept, and I saw his tongue sticking out, all black. I touched
him and he was already hard, like there was cement under his
fur.

KID

Dead?

AL

My dad said he must have eaten some poison.

Kid jumps to his feet.

KID

Your dad's a fucking asshole!

AL

Why?!

KID

He should have taken him to the vet! I don't care what time it
was! He was your dog, Al!

*Before Kid can turn away, Al sees the flash of tears in his eyes. Kid
grabs his shotgun and marches across the meadow towards the woods.
Al moves quickly to follow him.*

Kid suddenly screams and fires his shotgun repeatedly into the earth beside him. The blasts echo loudly across the meadow.

EXT. CIRCLE RENT-A-CAR. DAY. LATER

The camera is close on a familiar cluster of road signs, reading NORTH *and* SOUTH, EAST *and* WEST. *Pan as Kid's convertible enters frame and pulls into the Circle Rent-a-Car from where Al rented his car. Doris can be seen behind the counter.*

> AL
>
> Good, they're open.

Al glances over at Kid slouched despondently behind the wheel.

> AL
>
> I'll be right out.

> KID
>
> Whatever.

Al hesitates a moment then gets out and enters the rental office.

INT. CIRCLE RENT-A-CAR. DAY. LATER

Doris stares skeptically across the counter at Al.

> DORIS
>
> How did you lose them, Mr Fountain?

> AL
>
> Carelessness, I'm afraid, Doris.

> DORIS
>
> And where is the car now?

> AL
>
> Oh, it's safe and sound. It's at my friend's house; a few miles outside of town.

> DORIS
>
> Well, I'm going to have to charge you a twenty-five-dollar key replacement fee.

                                AL

Fair enough.

*Al removes twenty-five dollars from his bonus envelope. As he hands it
to Doris he glances out the window.*

Camera moves into a CU *of Kid sitting in dejection staring moodily at
nothing.*

                              DORIS

I hope for your sake you don't lose these.

Al does not answer. Camera moves into a CU *of him as he continues
staring out at Kid.*

Mr Fountain? Mr Fountain.

CU *of Doris's hand holding a set of car keys on a string attached to a
paper tag marked: 'Circle: Substitute Set 1225A'.*

                                AL

Hold on, Doris. You just said something very, very smart.
Why should I spend my last two days here worrying about
losing keys? Especially since my friend has a car. I'm going to
give you directions and what I'd like you to do is deliver these
keys to me bright and early Thursday morning.

                              DORIS

We don't have a key delivery service, Mr Fountain.

                                AL

Oh, I see. But if you did I'm sure there would be a key
delivery fee. Am I right?

*Al slips a fifty-dollar bill out of his bonus envelope. Doris stares at it in
non-committal suspicion.*

EXT. CIRCLE RENT-A-CAR. DAY. LATER

*The camera follows Al out of the rental office and into Kid's convertible.
Kid is surprised at Al's somber look.*

                               KID

What's the matter?

                               149

AL

Just my luck; someone broke in this morning and stole all the goddam keys.

KID

You're kiddin' me. What about them key codes you told me about?

AL

The bastard stole them too. Soonest they can get me another set is Thursday morning.

KID

What are you going to do?

AL

Check back into my hotel I guess.

There is a brief pause. Kid stares across the highway, not looking at Al as he speaks.

KID

I suppose you could stay at my place.

AL

I appreciate that, Kid, but I'll only stay at your place on one condition; you let me buy some food.

KID

I got food.

AL

Yeah, but I thought maybe we could do a little Fourth of July thing. Barbecue a chicken, make some hamburgers. You like corn on the cob?

KID

Are you kiddin'? that's Nature's perfect food.

AL

Good; chicken, hamburgers, corn on the cob . . .

KID

Beer, jelly donuts.

AL

Watermelon.

                           KID

Fireworks.

                           AL

Hey, that's not a bad idea. We'll get some sparklers.

                           KID

Sparklers?! Are you fuckin' crazy?! I got a whole box of
fireworks, man. Real ones!

                           AL

I'm afraid those are illegal, Kid.

*Kid suddenly laughs and peels rubber out of the Circle parking lot. One
of his hubcaps flies off and rolls down the street.*

INT. SUPERMARKET. DAY. LATER

*Al and Kid move down the aisle of a huge rural supermarket. Red,
white and blue banners and signs announce the approaching holiday.*

*Al pushes the cart, already filled with packages of chicken, beer, ground
beef, watermelon, corn, potato chips.*

                           AL

What about breakfast supplies, Kid? We're running a little
low.

                           KID

Good idea.

Kid stares in surprise as Al loads twenty bags of Oreos into the cart.

                           KID

What're you doing?

                           AL

My treat, Kid. What else do you need? Luncheon meats?

                           KID

Yeah. And Jelly donuts.

As Al and Kid quickly round the far end of the aisle, they almost ram

*two young women with the cart. Purlene and Floatie are both fairly
attractive but time and small-town life have given them some rough
edges. Floatie is crying quietly. Kid stops and stares at her. Before she
can turn away she reveals a small birthmark on the side of her face. It is
faintly purple and shaped roughly like a bird.*

PURLENE

What the hell are you looking at?

KID

Nothing.

PURLENE

Then get the fuck out of here.

*Kid suddenly pulls a package of fancy paper dinner napkins off the
shelf. He rips them open and hands a napkin to Floatie. Floatie takes it
and dabs at her eyes.*

FLOATIE

Thanks.

KID

Don't mention it.

152

Floatie meets Al's eyes for a moment then looks away self-consciously.

EXT. SUPERMARKET PARKING LOT

As Al and Kid wheel their cart out of the supermarket they are surprised to see groups of people rushing toward the far end of the parking lot. Cars and trucks have pulled off the road beside a tattered, fading billboard showing a single hamburger sizzling over a fire. A crowd has gathered, everyone staring up at the billboard. Two policemen stand beside their squad car, its bubble lights flashing.

The crowd is made up of people of all ages, many with cameras and video recorders. A local TV news crew is filming. Kid yells to a father hurrying his family past the car.

> KID
>
> Hey, bud! What's goin' on?

> FATHER
>
> Someone saw Jesus on that sign!

> KID
>
> Where?

> FATHER
>
> In the fire! Right below the hamburger!

The father points quickly and runs off after his family. Al and Kid move closer and stare hard at the billboard. The camera moves toward the faded, peeling sign until the hamburger fills the frame.

> KID
>
> You see anything, Al?

> AL
>
> No.

> KID
>
> Me neither. Damn, I always just miss those things.

EXT. KID'S TRAILER. CAMPFIRE. NIGHT

CU: *TV set; a wrestling match fills the screen. Uncle Samson grapples with Saddam Insane, a dark-skinned Arab with a big black mustache.*

153

Kid watches tensely from his recliner, a box of jelly donuts opened beside him.

Al sits inside the trailer talking on the phone.

> AL
>
> We got back to the plant today and found some vandals had broken in while we were gone and did some minor damage to the turbine. So, I'm afraid I'm going to be delayed another day, Deb.

CUT TO: *Deb holding the phone in silence. Finally she speaks.*

> DEB
>
> Let me get this straight. First you said you'd be home on the fifth. Then you said the third. Then it was the fourth. And now, after all this talk about getting home early, once again you tell me you won't be home till the fifth.

> AL
>
> That's correct, Deb; early afternoon on the fifth. And I just want to say I really look forward to seeing you.

Kid leaps out of his broken recliner chair and screams in outrage as Saddam gives Sam a vicious 'kick' in the balls. Saddam then advances on the unconscious Sam with a huge curved sword, intent on cutting his hair.

> DEB
>
> Well, Al, I guess I'll see you on the fifth then, or the sixth or the tenth or the eighth or whenever the hell you feel like coming home. Here is your son.

Deb hands the phone to Bobby and walks out of the room. Bobby stands hesitantly, the huge set of flashcards dangling listlessly under his arm.

> AL
>
> Hi, Bob. Your mom's in a bad mood?

Sound of a door slamming.

> BOBBY
>
> I think so.

AL

I'll tell you what then, Bob. I've only got a second here, and I
know you're busy so let's just do an easy one. What's twelve
times two?

*Bobby doesn't move; his entire being is mired in despair and
hopelessness. Al's voice is heard through the phone.*

(*voice-over*)
Bob? Come on. That's an easy one. Twelve times two.

BOBBY

I don't know.

The cards fall from Bobby's arm and he quietly starts crying.

AL
(*startled*)
Bob, what are you doing? Are you crying?

BOBBY

No sir.

He most definitely is.

AL

Hey, hey come on now, Bob. Pull yourself together. Nothing
to be upset about; you're doing fine. Just keep at those
flashcards and you'll be alright. OK. Bob? Bob?

BOBBY
(*sniffling*)

OK.

CUT TO: *Al sitting motionless, holding the phone to his ear in silence.*

EXT. KID'S TRAILER. CAMPFIRE. NIGHT. LATER

QUICK CUT TO: *Uncle Samson leaping off the top rope and landing on
the prone Saddam's head with both booted feet. Then Sam picks up
Saddam by his mustache and swings him completely out of the ring.
The crowd goes wild, chanting 'Sam! Sam! Uncle Sam!'*

Al walks out of the trailer just as the match ends.

KID

That fuckin diaperhead kicked Sam in the balls!

AL

Hurt bad?

KID

Are you kidding?! Almost killed him. He's not Superman, Al. He feels it just like you or me.

Al's attention is suddenly drawn to the TV, where a Newscaster is presenting the top local news story.

NEWSCASTER

A miracle occurred today, according to Willard Snarp of Drip Rock, who claims to have seen the face of Jesus on a billboard outside the Big Lucky Shopping Center on Route 17.

CUT TO: *a shot of Willard Snarp standing in front of the billboard; crowds of people mill around him.*

WILLARD

I saw it. It's Jesus alright; dressed in modern clothes, wearing a suit with a bowtie.

CUT TO: *a shot of the hamburger.*

NEWSCASTER

Religious experts from the Vatican will arrive on Monday to authenticate the sighting. In other religious news police today arrested a local minister, charging him with a brutal triple murder.

CUT TO: *news footage of Luvven and Wynelle Coddle being escorted into a police car, shots of the murder scene: a hand protruding from beneath a sheet.*

Police say Reverend Luvven and Wynelle Coddle of Neeterboro entered the home of Earl and Lindy Sykes last night and hacked them to death with a small ax. Their six-year-old daughter Mandy was also killed.

CUT TO: *a photo of the Sykes family.*

156

Neighbors told police the Sykes had recently withdrawn from Reverend Coddle's Church of Light.

CUT TO: *shot of a hand-cuffed Luvven Coddle moving right toward the camera. Just as he passes he looks up and stares out, as if looking Al right in the eye.*

Kid suddenly lunges out and punches off the TV.

> KID

Goddammit. Killin' a six-year-old girl. What the hell is wrong with people. Makes you feel like taking a machine-gun and really doing something . . .

Al and Kid sit in stunned silence. WIDE SHOT *of the yard. A single yellow light inside the trailer spills out on to Al and Kid sitting in the darkness. The moon slips from behind a cloud and casts milky blue light through the leaves. Al notices the closed lacquer box sitting in a moonbeam and reaches for it.*

> KID

Don't open that!

> AL

Why not?

> KID

You'll let the moonlight out. Come on, man; use your head.

Al sets the box back down. CU: *the box, gleaming mysteriously, half in the shadows.*

> AL

Let's get out of here.

> KID

What do you mean?

> AL

Don't you know a bar in town? Come on, I'll buy you a drink.

> KID

Good idea. I'm sick of sitting' around this place.

EXT. TOWN STREETS. NIGHT. LATER

Traveling shots of the car moving through town at night. The streets are deserted; fast-food places, gas stations; all closed. Eddie's Mix is in the tape deck.

EXT. BAMBI'S BAR. NIGHT. LATER

WIDE SHOT: *the exterior of Bambi's. It is a tiny, one-story building set back from a deserted road., A few red and yellow spotlights illuminate its crumbling façade and half-filled parking lot. Pitch darkness surrounds it on all sides.*

A few people, mostly men, lean against their cars drinking. Top 40 music drones from a cheap speaker, interrupted frequently by the loud crack of an insect being electrocuted in the hanging Bug Zapper.

The camera dollies closer as Kid introduces Al to two men.

> KID
> Hey Stinky, hey Barnett. This is a friend of mine, Al Fountain. Al's a nuclear engineer.

> AL
> Electrical, actually: field installation of Zeus Turbine Generators. What line of work are you in Stinky?

> STINKY
> Work at the car wash.

> AL
> Oh really? Doing what?

> STINKY
> Washing cars; what do you fuckin' think?

> AL
> Good. How about you, Barnett?

> BARNETT
> Cesspools. Got my own truck.

Kid reaches down and picks up a cheap disposable lighter from the pavement. It doesn't work when he tests it.

158

KID

This yours, Stinky?

STINKY

Nope.

Just then Wick's Chevy pulls into the parking lot still dragging its muffler. Al and Kid watch cautiously as Wick and Doob get out and move past them on their way into the bar.

KID

Hey, Wick. Hey, Doob. You see Jesus?

WICK

Fuck you.

Just then Stinky lights a cigarette and flicks the still-lit match away from him. CU: *the flaming match bouncing off Wick's leg and landing on the pavement by his shoe. Wick stops abruptly and whirls to face Kid.*

WICK

Are you fuckin' with me?!

KID

No, Wick! What's the matter?!

WICK

You threw another match at me!

KID

No, I didn't throw a match, Wick. Alls I got is a lighter.

Kid holds out the disposable lighter. Wick stares at it for a long moment as the parking lot grows quiet. Just as Kid smiles, Wick punches him hard in the face. Kid's head snaps back with a sickening crunch.

AL

Alright that's it, goddammit!

As Al lunges toward Wick, Doob suddenly punches him hard in the stomach. Al sinks into a crouch, gasping for air and trying to steady himself with one hand on the asphalt. Doob shoves him into the front of a car and his head hits hard against a headlight, cracking it.

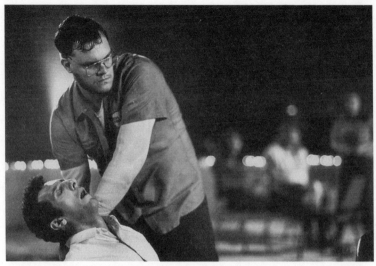

Dazed, Al tries to struggle to his feet. Through glazed eyes he sees Kid take a frantic swing at Wick. Wick steps easily aside and again punches Kid in the face, knocking him to his knees. Blood flows from his mouth to the asphalt. Wick casually positions himself behind Kid and gives him a vicious kick in the balls.

Al tries to scream in outrage but there is still no air in his lungs. Kid collapses face down on the asphalt and loses consciousness.

Wick walks up to Kid's fallen coonskin cap and kicks it out of his way. CU: *the cap flying across the black sky in slow-motion.*

EXT. KID'S TRAILER. NIGHT. LATER

Out of pitch darkness, car headlights suddenly wash over the face of the ceramic dwarf, standing with wide eyes and a goofy lop-sided grin.

Al steers Kid's car into the yard and kills the engine. Moving unsteadily himself he helps Kid, who is babbling incoherently, over to the fold-out couch. Al has a huge bump on his forehead. Kid's face is smeared with dried blood.

KID

Al, you go out in the woods and get some Blood Weed.

AL

What are you talking about, 'bloodweed?' Just be quite a
second.

KID

No, I'm just gonna catch my breath for minute then we'll
sneak into Wick's house when he's asleep and smear that shit
all over him. In his face; in his mouth, in his eyes. That's
right, right in his eyes, man. That way if he ever stops
bleeding that fucker's gonna be blind for the rest of his life!

AL

Kid. Come on now. Pull yourself together. Let me take a look
at you.

KID

I'm alright, Al. Now you get goin'. Take a flashlight; wear
some gloves.

AL

Listen to me, Kid. We're not going anywhere.

KID

You're not going to help me, Al?

AL

I'm trying to help you. Now cut this shit out.

KID

Alright, man. I'll do it myself.

*Kid suddenly lurches free and staggers towards the woods. Al moves
quickly and grabs his arm.*

AL

Kid, come on now. Calm down.

KID

Why aren't you going to help me, Al? I thought you were my
friend. You're not going to help me? Al? Al?

*Kid suddenly falls against Al, clutching him tightly like a frightened
child. Al sits startled for a moment then awkwardly returns the embrace.*

EXT. ROCK POOL. DAY

DISSOLVE *to the water of the rock pool; sunshine glinting off its gently moving surface.*

Al and Kid sit gloomily on the rocks; both in their underwear. Kid's face is cleaned up but bruised and swollen. Al's forehead has turned dark blue.

> KID
>
> What are you thinkin' about?

> AL
>
> Oh, I don't know. Maybe this whole trip of mine was just a big mistake, Kid.

Suddenly the silence is broken by the sound of someone coming out of the woods. Both Al and Kid look up to see Floatie appear on the other side of the pool. They both watch her make her way over the rocks toward a patch of sunshine. Suddenly she stops and picks up the underwear Kid found the day before.

> FLOATIE
>
> Hey, Purlene! Here's your underwear!

Just then Purlene appears out of the woods and takes the underwear from Floatie. Kid completely ignores Al, eagerly watching the two women undress to their bathing suits and lie down on a flat rock across the pool. After a moment Kid gets up and stretches leisurely, making sure the women see him. Then he dives awkwardly into the water. Al watches him swim over toward the women and he hears snatches of their dialogue.

> KID
>
> Could I ask you something? Were my legs straight going in?

> PURLENE
>
> No.

> KID
>
> Goddammit, gotta keep practicin' I guess. I got an Olympic tryout in a month.

Kid pulls himself out of the water and flops down beside Purlene and

Floatie. Al watches them out of the corner of his eye. A moment later Purlene laughs. Suddenly Kid turns and points at Al and they all stare at him.

                    KID
Hey Al! Come on over!

Al quickly shakes his head 'no'.

                    KID
Come on. They want to talk to you.

Reluctantly Al walks over, trying to be casual as he puts his hands over the crotch of his wet underwear.

Al, this is Purlene and Flighty.

                    AL
Nice to meet you.

                    KID
We saw them in the store yesterday, remember? What were you crying' about?

                  FLOATIE
Oh, I lost my job. It was a really good one too. I just, well, I only worked there a week and –

                    KID
They're sisters! Isn't that crazy?

                    AL
Sisters. Well, very nice.

                  PURLENE
Where are you from?

                    AL
Chicago.

                    KID
Al's a nuclear engineer.

                    AL
Electrical actually: field installation of Zeus Turbine Generators.

FLOATIE

Some people can give an electric shock just by looking at you.

Floatie's comment brings the conversation to a sudden halt. Kid stares at her inquisitively for a moment then turns to Purlene.

KID

What about you; you a swimsuit model?

PURLENE

What?

KID

You are, right?

PURLENE

Buddy, I work at Deever's Tire Service and I hate to say it, but I think it's time you came in and get your fucking wheels rebalanced.

Al suddenly laughs, followed a moment later by both Purlene and Floatie. Kid remains quite solemn.

KID

Alright, alright, go ahead laugh. But I'll tell you something; you used to be a cheerleader, didn't you?

PURLENE

In the fourth fucking grade.

KID

And your hair's not really blonde, is it?

PURLENE

Yes, it is.

FLOATIE

No, it isn't. She's a redhead. She's got a bright red bush.

PURLENE
(*slaps her hard*)

I can't believe you said that!

Kid turns and gives Al a solemn stare of reproof.

> KID

Alright Al, I'm not going to say anything.

> PURLENE

What's with you guys? You in a car wreck?

> KID

Naw, we got jumped last night over at Bambi's by four or five sailors.

> PURLENE

I've never seen sailors in Drip Rock.

> KID

Wasn't it sailors, Al?

> AL

No. They were marines, five of them.

> FLOATIE

That's a good movie; *The Green Berets*. Did anybody see that movie? I really liked it. John Wayne, Kim Darby. Some Japanese guy.

This time Floatie's remark brings the conversation to an abrupt, lengthy halt.

> KID

Damn, it's hot. I'm burnin' up.

> PURLENE

Jump in the water then, fireball.

> KID

No, but I might take my suit off.

> PURLENE

Looks like underwear to me.

> FLOATIE
> (*pointing at Al's wet underwear*)

He's wearin' underwear too, and you can see right through it.

> PURLENE

I noticed that.

KID

Alright, so we're wearin' underwear. We're just wearing them cause you're here. We always go naked.

PURLENE

So do we.

KID

Why don't you take your suits off now?

PURLENE

Don't feel like it.

She gets up.

KID

Where you going?

PURLENE

I'm going to jump off that rock. Is that alright with you?

KID
(*following her*)

Ever try it naked?

PURLENE

Listen, bonehead, I'm not taking my suit off. So just forget about it.

Purlene jumps into the pool, followed a moment later by Kid. Al and Floatie sit in a slightly uncomfortable silence. Floatie makes sure her birthmark faces away from Al.

FLOATIE

My name's Floatie, not Flighty.

AL

Oh, I see. Excuse me a second, Floatie. I've got to go check something.

Al gets up and returns to his original spot on the rocks, pausing to studiously scrutinize his watch. Floatie gets up without a word and jumps into the water to join Kid and Purlene.

AL

Al, if you don't want to prance around in your wet
underwear, you don't have to. It's your choice. 'Each man
must choose how he marches in the parade of Life.' Al
Fountain. Wednesday July 4. 1.05 p.m.

*Shots of Kid, Purlene and Floatie flying through the air. Underwater
shots: their bodies hitting the water in slow-motion; explosions of
bubbles, eyes clenched shut.*

EXT. KID'S TRAILER. CAMPFIRE. DAY

WIDE SHOT: *Kid's yard. Kid is inside the trailer looking for something.
Al kneels outside beside a fire blazing in a sturdy fireplace he has made
out of rocks.*

*Al seems quite, reflective, as he tends the chicken sizzling on the grill.
Nonetheless he has still arranged all his cooking supplies in neat order
around him. Ears of corn wrapped in tinfoil, a plate of well-shaped
hamburger covered with plastic wrap.*

Kid comes sauntering out with an old beat-up tape player.

KID

Smells good, Al. Hey, what's with the corn?

AL

Well, you didn't have a pot, Kid. So we'll just toss them in
the coals.

KID
(*amazed*)

They'll cook that way?

AL

Oh yeah. About fifteen or twenty minutes.

KID

Where's that weird tape of yours? The girls might like it.

AL

What girls?

167

KID

Purlene and Floatie. I invited 'em over for dinner.

AL

Why?

KID

Well, they weren't doin' anything. And Floatie's still feelin' a little low. She kind of likes you, Al.

AL

Does she?

KID

Yup, Purlene told me.

AL

Kid, let's get something squared away right now. I'm a married man. I don't make a habit of fooling around with every woman who 'kind of likes me'.

KID

Al, I'm glad to hear that, man. Really. Now, where's that tape?

AL

Look in the car.

EXT. KID'S TRAILER. DINING AREA. EVENING. LATER

Odd music is heard from Eddie's Mix. Al, Kid, Purlene and Floatie sit around the toy pool table eating. Both women have made a conscious effort to dress up.

FLOATIE

I really like your house. You've got a living room, a dining room, a kitchen area . . .

KID

Oh, yeah. but Al's gonna do a whole number here. He's gonna help me put in the this, the that, the swimming pool, 'cause Al's a nuclear engineer.
(*laughs*)
Al and I do porno. In our spare time, of course.

168

He guffaws as the two women look at him like he's an idiot.

> Come on, ladies. Got three more burgers cookin' over there.
> How 'bout it, Floatie? Purlene?

*Al returns to Floatie and takes her hand, leading her back to the fire.
The group begins dancing around the fire, with Kid alternately squirting
huge jets of lighter fluid into the flames.*

*Eddie's Mix blasts out of the cheap tape player. Kid pulls off his
buckskin shirt and leaps through the flames bare-chested. Surprisingly it
is Floatie who next removes her blouse, flinging it away from her almost
angrily. Purlene quickly follows her and then, a moment later, so does
Al.*

*Al appears a little self-conscious but whatever was in those pills Purlene
passed out is definitely taking effect. As he watches, Kid suddenly passes
through the flames in slow-motion, his body seemingly weightless.*

*A succession of shots of bodies floating through the flames. More and
more clothing is removed until everyone is in their underwear. Sweat
glistens on skin, the women's hair streams out behind them. The shots
will emphasize the bodies moving through space; flying.*

Extreme WIDE SHOT: *four naked figures leaping around a fire in front
of half a mobile home surrounded by dark forest.*

*As the song ends, Kid and Purlene disappear, leaving Al gazing into the
fire. Floatie's face appears through the flames, wavering in the heat.
They both move slowly toward each other.*

EXT. KID'S TRAILER. BACK YARD. NIGHT. LATER

*Al falls backwards on to the sofa-bed. Floatie's face hovers inches above
his. They kiss slowly. Al gently rolls her over and they begin to make
love.*

*The camera slowly drifts away from them, passing Kid and Purlene,
entangled in the Lazy Boy recliner. The camera continues on, moving
close to the ground through the shadows until it comes upon the old
lacquer box gleaming softly in a shaft of moonlight. Fade to black.*

EXT. KID'S TRAILER. BACKYARD. MORNING

The camera moves quickly along a wooded dirt road dappled with morning sunlight streaming through the trees. The camera pulls into Kid's driveway and stops.

CUT TO: *Doris, sitting at the wheel of her car, staring through the windshield in stunned astonishment.*

                    PURLENE
Not me. I got my jeans unbuttoned now.

                    KID
Let's see.

                    PURLENE
Get out of here, man. You're like a goddam dog.

                    FLOATIE
He is. Remember Stinky? That stray that slept in the garage?

                    PURLENE
With the one ear that never laid down?

                    FLOATIE
Don't he look like him? Same hair, same eyes.

                    KID
Well thanks. You all look pretty nice yourselves. Don't they, Al?

                    AL
                 (*remotely*)
Very nice.

                    FLOATIE
I never had corn cooked this way.

                    KID
That's Al; he made the corn and the chicken. But I cooked the burgers.

                    PURLENE
You boys would make some good husbands.

170

KID

We probably would.

PURLENE

Too bad we're not looking for any.

KID

Yeah, well we're not either. Besides Al's already married. Right, Al?

Al merely nods.

FLOATIE

You don't feel well?

AL

Actually, my head has started hurting me again.

PURLENE

Here, honey. Take one of these.

Purlene pulls a vial of white pills out of her pocket.

AL

What are they?

PURLENE

Just aspirin; with a little something extra.

Al takes a pill.

KID

I got a headache too.

PURLENE

Help yourself. Floatie?

FLOATIE

Yeah, I feel a headache comin' on.

Al watches with mild surprise as Kid, Floatie and Purlene all take pills.

Kid slips his arm around Purlene and whispers in her ear. She laughs loudly, slapping him so hard he falls off his chair. Al and Floatie sit quietly, staring down at their plates. Al suddenly gets up and goes over to the fire where he begins poking the coals in a very serious manner.

A moment later Floatie wanders away from the table. She lights a sparkler and walks slowly around the yard with it.

EXT. KID'S TRAILER. FRONT YARD. NIGHT. LATER

Kid lights the fuse of a small Roman candle then steps back as the brightly colored fountain of sparks erupts. His arm slips naturally around Purlene's waist and she leans comfortably against him.

Floatie sits alone on the fold-out couch. Al lies in the grass some distance away. He stares at the fireworks with intense fascination, frequently blinking and lightly shaking his head.

KID
Little better than fuckin' sparklers, huh, Al?

Al merely nods, mesmerized. He seems to be feeling the first effects of Pulene's 'pills'. Kid lights another Roman candle, holding it sideways, sending blazing spheres arcing across the yard to bounce off trees and the side of the mobile home.

The camera moves into an extreme CU *of Al, staring with sudden concentration at Kid leaping back from a lighted fuse. Kid moves slower and slower finally stopping in mid-stride just as the firework erupts.*

CUT TO: CU *of coffee running backwards out of a cup.*

CUT TO: MS *of a small boy on a bike, riding backwards.*

CUT TO: CU *of a gray hair falling in slow-motion.*

Just as the hair hits the floor Kid runs up to Al, who is quite amazed by these hallucinations.

> KID
>
> Feelin' alright, Al?

> AL
>
> Oh yeah, I feel fine. I just figured something out, Kid. This whole backwards phenomenon of mine started the day I noticed my first gray hair.

He stares at Kid.

> You see that, Kid? It's me; I'm trying to stop Time.

> KID
>
> That's too much, man. Wow. You don't like Floatie?

> AL
>
> What?

> KID
>
> She thinks you don't like her cause of that mark on her face.

> AL
>
> That's ridiculous. Where is she?

> KID
>
> Over on the couch.

> AL
>
> Alright, I'm going to go talk to her, Kid; let her know everything's fine here. OK? Thanks. You're alright, Kid. I mean it, you really are. So don't worry, I'm going over there now, and I'm going to get everything squared away.

Al slowly gets to his feet and drifts across the lawn toward Floatie, now alone again on the fold-out sofa.

EXT. KID'S TRAILER. BACK YARD. NIGHT. LATER

Al sits on the fold-out sofa a few feet away from Floatie. Kid and Purlene toss paper garbage into the growing fire. Eddie's Mix still plays.

AL

Where were you working, Floatie?

FLOATIE

I was in phone . . . sales.

AL

Oh, really? Office supplies, clothing catalogues?

FLOATIE

Sex.

AL

Excuse me?

FLOATIE

Phone sex. A company called Love Phone. You ever heard of it?

She hands Al a pink Love Phone card, identical to the others Al has seen. Al's surprise is obvious though he pretends to scrutinize the card with casual interest.

No, I'm afraid I haven't.

FLOATIE

It was the perfect job for me. I'm kind of a quiet person, Al. I like to just sit around and think up things, you know fantasies, not all of them about sex. I've got a whole bunch of stories in my mind about a Princess who can kill people just by looking at them. But she only does it to guys who try to hurt her 'cause there are a lot of nice guys out there. I talked to a lot of them on the phone.

Floatie turns and stares at Al. He returns her gaze for a moment before continuing.

AL

Why were you fired?

FLOATIE

They tried me for a week but guys kept hanging up on me. I guess I'm one of those kind of people that aren't sexy, even if it's just over the phone.

AL

Now hold on a second, Floatie. I think you're exaggerating a little bit there.

FLOATIE

What do you mean?

AL

Well, I think you're . . . sexy.

Floatie turns to Al again, her eyes betraying a mixture of suspicion and hope. Al stares back. Their bodies move towards each other a slow fraction of an inch. In the background, around the fire, Kid turns up the volume on the tape player and 'Carioca' by The Fireballs starts up. Just as Al is about to kiss Floatie, he suddenly lurches to his feet.

Everyone stares in amazement as Al breaks into a lurching, halfway professional tango step that carries him around the fire.

KID

Alright, Al! Shake that thing!

Doris slowly gets out of the car, wearing her hot pink Circle Rent-a-Car uniform, and regards the tableau before her.

She sees half a mobile home, surrounded by an assortment of lawn ornaments. She sees Al and Floatie lying outside naked on a fold-out bed. She sees Kid and Purlene curled up naked in a Lazy Boy recliner under a tree, Kid with his coonskin cap still on. Clothing as well as firework and picnic debris lies strewn all over the lawn.

Finally she walks slowly toward the fold-out bed and warily pokes Al's foot. His eyes slowly open.

DORIS

Mr Fountain?

AL

Good morning, Doris. How are you?

DORIS

I have the extra set of keys, Mr Fountain.

AL

Thank you. I won't get up because I'm not dressed. Just leave them on the bed.

Kid tumbles out of the chair and stands naked before Doris.

> **KID**
> Did you want to buy something, ma'am? I've got some birds,
> a giraffe and a beautiful rubber snake.

*Doris sets the extra keys on the pool table and backs slowly towards her
car. She stumbled over the ceramic dwarf standing in the grass behind
her.*

> I'm lettin' that go for about thirty-five.

*Doris gets in her car and drives away, staring back so hard she runs off
the road with a crash.*

EXT. KID'S TRAILER. DRIVEWAY. DAY. LATER

*Floatie gets into her car and starts it. Al, now dressed approaches her
window and rests his hand on the door. Purlene is in the passenger seat
locked in a kiss with Kid whose body is half in the window. Kid is
barefoot, wearing only his buckskin pants and his coonskin cap.*

> **FLOATIE**
> Well, it was nice to meet you, Al.

> **AL**
> You too, Floatie.

CU: *Floatie's hand. It shifts an inch so it is almost touching Al's. His
finger moves to touch her hand softly. For a moment it looks like they
will kiss. They don't.*

Purlene breaks the kiss with Kid.

> **PURLENE**
> Jesus, let me take a breath will you?

> **KID**
> Sorry, I just wanted something to remember you by.

> **PURLENE**
> What, are you leavin' the country?

> **KID**
> Nope, I'll be here. Why, you want to come over tonight?

I don't know. I'll tell you one thing; I'm not sleeping in a
goddam chair.

*Floatie pulls out of the driveway. Kid hangs on to the car until the last
moment before dropping off and somersaulting in the grass. Then he
stands up and stares back at Al for a long moment.*

INT. AL'S CAR. DAY. LATER

CU: *Al's back-up keys fitting into the ignition. They turn; the car starts.*

*Kid shifts nervously outside Al's window. Al too seems anxious and
uncomfortable.*

KID

There you go, Al. You're out of here.

AL

I guess so, Kid.

KID

Listen, If you're ever down this way again just drop in. OK?
Any time, I mean it.

AL

Will do, Kid. And you've got my number; if you ever get to
Chicago, give me a call.

KID

Alright, sure. Hey, I might get out there one day.

AL
(*pause*)

Well, goodbye, Kid.

KID

So long, Al.

*The two shake hands through the car window. Al withdraws his hand
and heads his car down the driveway.*

Hold on a second!

Kid runs up to the window and hands Al the closed lacquer box.

KID

Here, little momentum from your stay here.

AL

Well thanks, Kid. Thank you very much. You take care of yourself.

KID

Hey, you know me, Al.

Al's car slowly pulls away. Al's POV of Kid standing in front of his half-a-mobile home, grinning and waving goodbye.

INT. AL'S CAR. COUNTRY ROAD. DAY. LATER

Al drives along the dirt road. sunlight filtering through the trees washes across his face. He glances down at the box lying on the seat beside him. Shafts of sunlight rush over it.

AERIAL SHOT. CHICAGO. DAY. LATER

DISSOLVE: *the camera moves over the dense, urban sprawl of Chicago. Freeways, shopping malls, endless housing projects and office buildings.*

INT. FOUNTAIN HOME. DAY. LATER

DISSOLVE: *Framed by a window, Bobby paces in a tiny backyard holding his giant flashcards in both hands. A small rusting swingset tilts off-balance behind him. Suddenly Bobby stops and looks up as Al enters the frame and approaches him.*

Camera pulls back to reveal Deb standing at the window, looking out at Bobby and Al.

EXT. FOUNTAIN HOME. BACK YARD. DAY. LATER

Al and Bobby stand in the back yard, some distance apart. Both seem anxious and nervous.

AL

How's it going, Bob?

BOBBY

Good! I've them memorized, Dad. I only need about ten more minutes.

Al takes the flashcards from Bobby's hands.

AL

I'll tell you what, Bob. Why don't we just put these on hold for a moment? There's no rush here. I'll help you and we'll do them together sometime. OK?

Bobby stares at his father warily as he drops the flashcards on the grass and sit on one of the tiny swings.

AL

So, you had a good Fourth?

BOBBY

Yes sir.

AL

Good.

A long moment of strained silence passes before Al speaks again. He hands Bobby a small package.

Well, here's a little something, Bob.

Al stands and pauses for a moment before hesitantly placing his hand on Bobby's shoulder. Then he crosses the tiny lawn and re-enters the house, leaving Bobby standing in motionless confusion.

INT. FOUNTAIN HOME. BEDROOM. DAY. LATER

Deb turns away from the window as Al enters and begins unpacking his suitcase. The closed lacquer box sits on the bed.

DEB

How's he doing?

AL

We didn't get into it, Deb. I figured, what the hell, I just got home.

Deb watches Al unpack for a moment.

DEB

We can eat as soon as you're unpacked.

AL

A little early, isn't it?

DEB
(mildly surprised)

It's six. You always eat at six.

AL
(smiles)

That's right, I forgot. I'm Mr Clockwork.

Deb walks over and looks at Al more closely. She gently touches the bruise on his forehead.

DEB

I'm glad you're home, Al.

AL

Well, Deb; I'm glad to be home. I missed you.

They share a brief, but tender kiss. Then Al hands Deb the lacquer box.

I found this in the woods. I thought you could use if to keep
your jewelry in.

                              DEB
Thanks, Al.

*Deb lifts the lid and looks inside the box for a moment. She opens a
small compartment and to her surprise sees a set of car keys.*

                              DEB
Whose are these?

*Al looks up from the other side of the room. Camera begins to dolly in to
his startled face.*

Dolly in to Deb's face, staring at Al in mild curiosity.

Dolly in to a CU *of Deb's hand. In it are the 'lost' Circle Rent-a-Car
keys on their hot pink plastic medallion.*

EXT. FOUNTAIN HOME. BACK YARD. DAY. LATER

WIDE SHOT: *the back yard. Bobby runs a few feet away from a
firework he has just lit the fuse of. Beside him is the now opened package
his father gave him.*

*Smoke and sparks from a firework rise on slow-motion, partially
obscuring Bobby. He kneels and stares at the firework in solemn
fascination. The smoke and shooting sparks fill the frame.*

DISSOLVE TO: *blue. End credits.*